Harvard Business Review

ON

MANAGING DIVERSITY

THE HARVARD BUSINESS REVIEW PAPERBACK SERIES

The series is designed to bring today's managers and professionals the fundamental information they need to stay competitive in a fast-moving world. From the preeminent thinkers whose work has defined an entire field to the rising stars who will redefine the way we think about business, here are the leading minds and landmark ideas that have established the *Harvard Business Review* as required reading for ambitious businesspeople in organizations around the globe.

Other books in the series:

Harvard Business Review

ON

MANAGING DIVERSITY

A HARVARD BUSINESS REVIEW PAPERBACK

The *Harvard Business Review* articles in this collection are available as
individual reprints. Discounts apply to quantity purchases. For information and ordering, please contact Customer Service, Harvard Business
School Publishing, Boston, MA 02163. Telephone: (617) 783-7500 or
(800) 988-0886, 8 A.M. to 6 P.M. Eastern Time, Monday through Friday.
Fax: (617) 783-7555, 24 hours a day. E-mail: custserv@hbsp.harvard.edu

Library of Congress Cataloging-in-Publication Data
Harvard business review on managing diversity.
        p.   cm. — (A Harvard business review paperback)
     Includes bibliographical references and index.
     ISBN 1-57851-700-1 (alk. paper)
     1. Diversity in the workplace.   2. Personnel management.   I. Title:
Managing diversity.   II. Harvard Business School Press.   III. Harvard
business review.   IV. Harvard business review paperback series.
HF5549.5.M5 H369   2002
658.3´008—dc21   2001039852
                                                                                CIP

*The paper used in this publication meets the requirements of the Ameri-
can National Standard for Permanence of Paper for Publications and
Documents in Libraries and Archives Z39.48-1992.*

Contents

Harvard Business Review

ON

MANAGING DIVERSITY

From Affirmative Action to Affirming Diversity

R. ROOSEVELT THOMAS, JR.

Executive Summary

AFFIRMATIVE ACTION IS based on a set of 30-year-old premises that badly need revising. White males are no longer dominant at every level of the corporation (statistically, they are merely the largest of many minorities), while decades of attack have noticeably weakened the racial and gender prejudices.

At the intake level, affirmative action quite effectively sets the stage for a workplace that is gender-, culture-, and color-blind. But minorities and women tend to stagnate, plateau, or quit when they fail to move up the corporate ladder, and everyone's dashed hopes lead to corporate frustration and a period of embarrassed silence, usually followed by a crisis—and more recruitment. Some companies have repeated this cycle three or four times.

The problem is that our traditional image of assimilation differences—the American melting pot—is no longer valid. It's a seller's market for skill, and the people business has to attract are refusing to be melted down. So companies are faced with the task of managing *unassimilated* diversity and getting from it the same commitment, quality, and profit they once got from a homogenous work force.

To reach this goal, we need to work not merely toward culture- and color-blindness but also toward an openly multicultural workplace that taps the full potential of every employee without artificial programs, standards, or barriers. The author gives his own ten guidelines for learning to manage diversity by learning to understand and modify your company's culture, vision, assumptions, models, and systems.

Sooner or later, affirmative action will die a natural death. Its achievements have been stupendous, but if we look at the premises that underlie it, we find assumptions and priorities that look increasingly shopworn. Thirty years ago, affirmative action was invented on the basis of these five appropriate premises:

1. Adult, white males make up something called the U.S. business mainstream.

2. The U.S. economic edifice is a solid, unchanging institution with more than enough space for everyone.

3. Women, blacks, immigrants, and other minorities should be allowed in as a matter of public policy and common decency.

4. Widespread racial, ethnic, and sexual prejudice keeps them out.

5. Legal and social coercion are necessary to bring about the change.

Today all five of these premises need revising. Over the past six years, I have tried to help some 15 companies learn how to achieve and manage diversity, and I have seen that the realities facing us are no longer the realities affirmative action was designed to fix.

To begin with, more than half the U.S. work force now consists of minorities, immigrants, and women, so white, native-born males, though undoubtedly still dominant, are themselves a statistical minority. In addition, white males will make up only 15% of the increase in the work force over the next ten years. The so-called mainstream is now almost as diverse as the society at large.

More than half the U.S. work force now consists of minorities, immigrants, and women.

Second, while the edifice is still big enough for all, it no longer seems stable, massive, and invulnerable. In fact, American corporations are scrambling, doing their best to become more adaptable, to compete more successfully for markets and labor, foreign and domestic, and to attract all the talent they can find. (See the end of this article for what a number of U.S. companies are doing to manage diversity.)

Third, women and minorities no longer need a boarding pass, they need an upgrade. The problem is not getting them in at the entry level; the problem is making better use of their potential at every level, especially in middle-management and leadership positions. This is no longer simply a question of common decency, it is a question of business survival.

Fourth, although prejudice is hardly dead, it has suffered some wounds that may eventually prove fatal. In the meantime, American businesses are now filled with progressive people—many of them minorities and women themselves—whose prejudices, where they still exist, are much too deeply suppressed to interfere with recruitment. The reason many companies are still wary of minorities and women has much more to do with education and perceived qualifications than with color or gender. Companies are worried about productivity and well aware that minorities and women represent a disproportionate share of the undertrained and undereducated.

Fifth, coercion is rarely needed at the recruitment stage. There are very few places in the United States today where you could dip a recruitment net and come up with nothing but white males. Getting hired is not the problem—women and blacks who are seen as having the necessary skills and energy can get *into* the work force relatively easily. It's later on that many of them plateau and lose their drive and quit or get fired. It's later on that their managers' inability to manage diversity hobbles them and the companies they work for.

In creating these changes, affirmative action had an essential role to play and played it very well. In many companies and communities it still plays that role. But affirmative action is an artificial, transitional intervention intended to give managers a chance to correct an imbalance, an injustice, a mistake. Once the numbers mistake has been corrected, I don't think affirmative action alone can cope with the remaining long-term task of creating a work setting geared to the upward mobility of all kinds of people, including white males. It is difficult for affirmative action to influence upward mobility even in the short run, primarily because it is perceived to conflict with the meritocracy we favor. For this reason, affirmative action is a red flag to every individual who feels unfairly passed over and a stigma for those who appear to be its beneficiaries.

Moreover, I doubt very much that individuals who reach top positions through affirmative action are effective models for younger members of their race or sex. What, after all, do they model? A black vice president who got her job through affirmative action is not necessarily a model of how to rise through the corporate meritocracy. She may be a model of how affirmative action can work for the people who find or put themselves in the right place at the right time.

If affirmative action in upward mobility meant that no person's competence and character would ever be overlooked or undervalued on account of race, sex, ethnicity, origins, or physical disability, then affirmative action would be the very thing we need to let every corporate talent find its niche. But what affirmative action means in practice is an unnatural focus on one group, and what it means too often to too many employees is that someone is playing fast and loose with standards in order to favor that group. Unless we are to compromise our standards, a thing no competitive company can even contemplate, upward mobility for minorities and women should always be a question of pure competence and character unmuddled by accidents of birth.

And that is precisely why we have to learn to manage diversity—to move beyond affirmative action, not to repudiate it. Some of what I have to say may strike some readers—mostly those with an ax to grind—as directed

at the majority white males who hold most of the
decision-making posts in our economy. But I am speaking to all managers, not just white males, and I certainly
don't mean to suggest that white males somehow stand
outside diversity. White males are as odd and as normal
as anyone else.

The Affirmative Action Cycle

If you are managing diverse employees, you should ask
yourself this question: Am I fully tapping the potential
capacities of everyone in my department? If the answer
is no, you should ask yourself this follow-up: Is this failure hampering my ability to meet performance standards? The answer to this question will undoubtedly
be yes.

Think of corporate management for a moment as an
engine burning pure gasoline. What's now going into the
tank is no longer just gas, it has an increasing percentage
of, let's say, methanol. In the beginning, the engine will
still work pretty well, but by
and by it will start to sputter,
and eventually it will stall.
Unless we rebuild the engine,
it will no longer burn the fuel
we're feeding it. As the work
force grows more and more
diverse at the intake level, the
talent pool we have to draw on for supervision and management will also grow increasingly diverse. So the question is: Can we burn this fuel? Can we get maximum corporate power from the diverse work force we're now
drawing into the system?

The wrong question: "How are we doing on race relations?" The right question: "Is this a workplace where 'we' is everyone?"

Affirmative action gets blamed for failing to do things
it never could do. Affirmative action gets the new fuel

into the tank, the new people through the front door. Something else will have to get them into the driver's seat. That something else consists of enabling people, in this case minorities and women, to perform to their potential. This is what we now call managing diversity. Not appreciating or leveraging diversity, not even necessarily under-standing it. Just managing diversity in such a way as to get from a heterogeneous work force the same productivity, commitment, quality, and profit that we got from the old homogeneous work force.

The correct question today is not "How are we doing on race relations?" or "Are we promoting enough minority people and women?" but rather "Given the diverse work force I've got, am I getting the productivity, does it work as smoothly, is morale as high, as if every person in the company was the same sex and race and nationality?" Most answers will be, "Well, no, of course not!" But why shouldn't the answer be, "You bet!"?

When we ask how we're doing on race relations, we inadvertently put our finger on what's wrong with the question and with the attitude that underlies affirmative action. So long as racial and gender equality is something we grant to minorities and women, there will be no racial and gender equality. What we must do is create an environment where no one is advantaged or disadvantaged, an environment where "we" is everyone. What the traditional approach to diversity did was to create a cycle of crisis, action, relaxation, and disappointment that companies repeated over and over again without ever achieving more than the barest particle of what they were after.

Affirmative action pictures the work force as pipeline and reasons as follows: "If we can fill the pipeline with *qualified* minorities and women, we can solve our upward mobility problem. Once recruited, they will perform in

accordance with our promotional criteria and move naturally up our regular developmental ladder. In the past,
where minorities and women have failed to progress, they
were simply unable to meet our performance standards.
Recruiting qualified people will enable us to avoid special
programs and reverse discrimination."

This pipeline perspective generates a self-perpetuat-
ing, self-defeating, recruitment-oriented cycle with six
stages:

1. *Problem Recognition.* The first time through the
   cycle, the problem takes this form—We need more
   minorities and women in the pipeline. In later itera-
   tions, the problem is more likely to be defined as a
   need to retain and promote minorities and women.

2. *Intervention.* Management puts the company into
   what we may call an Affirmative Action Recruitment
   Mode. During the first cycle, the goal is to recruit
   minorities and women. Later, when the cycle is
   repeated a second or third time and the challenge
   has shifted to retention, development, and promotion, the goal is to recruit *qualified* minorities and
   women. Sometimes, managers indifferent or blind to
   possible accusations of reverse discrimination will
   institute special training, tracking, incentive, mentoring, or sponsoring programs for minorities and
   women.

3. *Great Expectations.* Large numbers of minorities and
   women have been recruited, and a select group has
   been promoted or recruited at a higher level to serve
   as highly visible role models for the newly recruited
   masses. The stage seems set for the natural progression of minorities and women up through the

pipeline. Management leans back to enjoy the fruits of its labor.

4. *Frustration.* The anticipated natural progression fails to occur. Minorities and women see themselves plateauing prematurely. Management is upset (and embarrassed) by the failure of its affirmative action initiative and begins to resent the impatience of the new recruits and their unwillingness to give the company credit for trying to do the right thing. Depending on how high in the hierarchy they have plateaued, alienated minorities and women either leave the company or stagnate.

5. *Dormancy.* All remaining participants conspire tacitly to present a silent front to the outside world. Executives say nothing because they have no solutions. As for those women and minorities who stayed on, calling attention to affirmative action's failures might raise doubts about their qualifications. Do they deserve their jobs, or did they just happen to be in the right place at the time of an affirmative action push? So no one complains, and if the company has a good public relations department, it may even wind up with a reputation as a good place for women and minorities to work.

If questioned publicly, management will say things like "Frankly, affirmative action is not currently an issue," or "Our numbers are okay," or "With respect to minority representation at the upper levels, management is aware of this remaining challenge."

In private and off the record, however, people say things like "Premature plateauing is a problem, and we don't know what to do," and "Our top people don't seem to be interested in finding a solution," and "There's plenty of racism and sexism around this place—whatever you may hear."

6. *Crisis.* Dormancy can continue indefinitely, but it is usually broken by a crisis of competitive pressure, governmental intervention, external pressure from a special interest group, or internal unrest. One company found that its pursuit of a Total Quality program was hampered by the alienation of minorities and women. Senior management at another corporation saw the growing importance of minorities in their customer base and decided they needed minority participation in their managerial ranks. In another case, growing expressions of discontent forced a break in the conspiracy of silence even after the company had received national recognition as a good place for minorities and women to work.

Whatever its cause, the crisis fosters a return to the Problem Recognition phase, and the cycle begins again. This time, management seeks to explain the shortcomings of the previous affirmative action push and usually concludes that the problem is recruitment. This assessment by a top executive is typical: "The managers I know are decent people. While they give priority to performance, I do not believe any of them deliberately block minorities or women who are qualified for promotion. On the contrary, I suspect they bend over backward to promote women and minorities who give some indication of being qualified.

"However, they believe we simply do not have the necessary talent within those groups, but because of the constant complaints they have heard about their deficiencies in affirmative action, they feel they face a no-win situation. If they do not promote, they are obstructionists. But if they promote people who are unqualified, they hurt performance and deny promotion to other employees unfairly. They can't win. The answer, in my mind, must be an ambitious new recruitment effort to bring in quality people."

And so the cycle repeats. Once again blacks, Hispanics, women, and immigrants are dropped into a previously homogeneous, all-white, all-Anglo, all-male, all native-born environment, and the burden of cultural change is placed on the newcomers. There will be new expectations and a new round of frustration, dormancy, crisis, and recruitment.

Ten Guidelines for Learning to Manage Diversity

The traditional American image of diversity has been assimilation: the melting pot, where ethnic and racial differences were standardized into a kind of American puree. Of course, the melting pot is only a metaphor. In real life, many ethnic and most racial groups retain their individuality and express it energetically. What we have is perhaps some kind of American mulligan stew; it is certainly no puree.

At the workplace, however, the melting pot has been more than a metaphor. Corporate success has demanded a good deal of conformity, and employees have voluntarily abandoned most of their ethnic distinctions at the company door.

Now those days are over. Today the melting pot is the wrong metaphor even in business, for three good reasons. First, if it ever was possible to melt down Scotsmen and Dutchmen and Frenchmen into an indistinguishable broth, you can't do the same with blacks, Asians, and women. Their differences don't melt so easily. Second, most people are no longer willing to be melted down, not even for eight hours a day—and it's a seller's market for skills.

What managers fear is a lowering of standards. But in a diverse work force, competence counts more than ever.

Third, the thrust of today's nonhierarchical, flexible, collaborative management requires a ten- or twenty-fold increase in our tolerance for individuality.

So companies are faced with the problem of surviving in a fiercely competitive world with a work force that consists and will continue to consist of *unassimilated diversity*. And the engine will take a great deal of tinkering to burn that fuel.

What managers fear from diversity is a lowering of standards, a sense that "anything goes." Of course, standards must not suffer. In fact, competence counts more than ever. The goal is to manage diversity in such a way as to get from a diverse work force the same productivity we once got from a homogeneous work force, and to do it without artificial programs, standards—or barriers.

Managing diversity does not mean controlling or containing diversity, it means enabling every member of your work force to perform to his or her potential. It means getting from employees, first, everything we have a right to expect, and, second—if we do it well—everything they have to give. If the old homogeneous work force performed dependably at 80% of its capacity, then the first result means getting 80% from the new heterogeneous work force too. But the second result, the icing on the cake, the unexpected upside that diversity can perhaps give as a bonus, means 85% to 90% from every-one in the organization.

For the moment, however, let's concentrate on the basics of how to get satisfactory performance from the new diverse work force. There are few adequate models. So far, no large company I know of has succeeded in managing diversity to its own satisfaction. But any num-ber have begun to try.

On the basis of their experience, here are my ten guidelines:

1. *Clarify Your Motivation.* A lot of executives are not sure why they should want to learn to manage diversity. Legal compliance seems like a good reason. So does com-munity relations. Many executives believe they have a social and moral responsibility to employ minorities and women. Others want to placate an internal group or pacify an outside organization. None of these are bad reasons, but none of them are business reasons, and given the nature and scope of today's competitive chal-lenges, I believe only business reasons will supply the necessary long-term motivation. In any case, it is the business reasons I want to focus on here.

In business terms, a diverse work force is not some-thing your company ought to have; it's something your company does have, or soon will have. Learning to man-age that diversity will make you more competitive.

2. *Clarify Your Vision.* When managers think about a diverse work force, what do they picture? Not publicly, but in the privacy of their minds?

One popular image is of minorities and women clus-tering on a relatively low plateau, with a few of them trickling up as they become assimilated into the pre-vailing culture. Of course, they enjoy good salaries and benefits, and most of them accept their status, appreci-ate the fact that they are doing better than they could do somewhere else, and are proud of the achievements of their race or sex. This is reactionary thinking, but it's a lot more common than you might suppose.

Another image is what we might call "heightened sensitivity." Members of the majority culture are sensitive to the demands of minorities and women for upward mobility and recognize the advantages of fully utilizing them. Minorities and women work at all levels of the corporation, but they are the recipients of generosity and know it. A few years of this second-class status drives most of them away and compromises the effectiveness of those that remain. Turnover is high.

Then there is the coexistence-compromise image. In the interests of corporate viability, white males agree to recognize minorities and women as equals. They bargain and negotiate their differences. But the win-lose aspect of the relationship preserves tensions, and the compromises reached are not always to the company's competitive advantage.

"Diversity and equal opportunity" is a big step up. It presupposes that the white male culture has given way to one that respects difference and individuality. The problem is that minorities and women will accept it readily as their operating image, but many white males, consciously or unconsciously, are likely to cling to a vision that leaves them in the driver's seat. A vision gap of this kind can be a difficulty.

In my view, the vision to hold in your own imagination and to try to communicate to all your managers and employees is an image of fully tapping the human resource potential of every member of the work force. This vision sidesteps the question of equality, ignores the tensions of coexistence, plays down the uncomfortable realities of difference, and focuses instead on individual enablement. It doesn't say, "Let *us* give *them* a chance." It assumes a diverse work force that includes us and them. It says, "Let's create an environment where everyone will do their best work."

Several years ago, an industrial plant in Atlanta with a highly diverse work force was threatened with closing unless productivity improved. To save their jobs, everyone put their shoulders to the wheel and achieved the results they needed to stay open. The senior operating manager was amazed.

For years he had seen minorities and women plateauing disproportionately at the lower levels of the organization, and he explained that fact away with two rationalizations. "They haven't been here that long," he told himself. And "This is the price we pay for being in compliance with the law."

When the threat of closure energized this whole group of people into a level of performance he had not imagined possible, he got one fleeting glimpse of people working up to their capacity. Once the crisis was over, everyone went back to the earlier status quo—white males driving and everyone else sitting back, looking on—but now there was a difference. Now, as he put it himself, he had been to the mountaintop. He knew that what he was getting from minorities and women was nowhere near what they were capable of giving. And he wanted it, crisis or no crisis, all the time.

3. *Expand Your Focus.* Managers usually see affirmative action and equal employment opportunity as centering on minorities and women, with very little to offer white males. The diversity I'm talking about includes not only race, gender, creed, and ethnicity but also age, background, education, function, and personality differences. The objective not to assimilate minorities and women

into dominant white male culture but to create a dominant heterogeneous culture.

The culture that dominates the United States socially and politically is heterogeneous, and works by giving its citizens the liberty to achieve their potential. Channeling that potential, once achieved, is an individual right but still a national concern. Something similar applies in the workplace, where the keys to success are individual ability and a corporate destination. Managing disparate talents to achieve common goals is what companies learned to do when they set their sights on, say, Total Quality. The secrets of managing diversity are much the same.

4. *Audit Your Corporate Culture.* If the goal not to assimilate diversity into the dominant culture but rather to build a culture that can digest unassimilated diversity, then you had better start by figuring out what your present culture looks like. Since what we're talking about here is the body of unspoken and unexamined assumptions, values, and mythologies that make your world go round, this kind of cultural audit is impossible to conduct without outside help. It's a research activity, done mostly with in-depth interviews and a lot of listening at the water cooler.

The notion that the cream will rise to the top is nonsense. Cream gets pulled or pushed to the top.

The operative corporate assumptions you have to identify and deal with are often inherited from the company's founder. "If we treat everyone as a member of the family, we will be successful" is not uncommon. Nor is its corollary "Father Knows Best."

Another widespread assumption, probably absorbed from American culture in general, is that "cream will rise to the top." In most companies, what passes for cream rising to the top is actually cream being pulled or pushed to the top by an informal system of mentoring and sponsorship.

Corporate culture is a kind of tree. Its roots are assumptions about the company and about the world. Its branches, leaves, and seeds are behavior. You can't change the leaves without changing the roots, and you can't grow peaches on an oak. Or rather, with the proper grafting, you *can* grow peaches an oak, but they come out an awful lot like acorns—small and hard and not much fun to eat. So if you want to grow peaches, you have to make sure the tree's roots are peach friendly.

5. *Modify Your Assumptions.* The real problem with this corporate culture tree is that every time you go to make changes in the roots, you run into terrible opposition. Every culture, including corporate culture, has root guards that turn out in force every time you threaten a basic assumption.

Take the family assumption as an example. Viewing the corporation as a family suggests not only that father knows best; it also suggests that sons will inherit the business, that daughters should stick to doing the company dishes, and that if Uncle Deadwood doesn't perform, we'll put him in the chimney corner and feed him for another 30 years regardless. Each assumption has its constituency and its defenders. If we say to Uncle Deadwood, "Yes, you did good work for 10 years, but years 11 and 12 look pretty bleak; we think it's time we helped you find another chimney," shock waves will travel through the company as every family-oriented employee draws a sword to defend the sacred concept of guaranteed jobs.

But you have to try. A corporation that wants to create an environment with no advantages or disadvantages for any group cannot allow the family assumption to remain in place. It must be labeled dishonest mythology.

Sometimes the dishonesties are more blatant. When I asked a white male middle manager how promotions were handled in his company, he said, "You need leadership capability, bottom-line results, the ability to work with people, and compassion." Then he paused and smiled. "That's what they say. But down the hall there's a guy we call Captain Kickass. He's ruthless, mean-spirited, and he steps on people. That's the behavior they really value. Forget what they say."

In addition to the obvious issue of hypocrisy, this example also raises a question of equal opportunity. When I asked this young middle manager if he thought minorities and women could meet the Captain Kickass standard, he said he thought they probably could. But the opposite argument can certainly be made. Whether we're talking about blacks in an environment that is predominantly white, whites in one predominantly black, or women in one predominantly male, the majority culture will not readily condone such tactics from a member of a minority. So the corporation with the unspoken kickass performance standard has at least one criterion that will hamper the upward mobility of minorities and women.

Another destructive assumption is the melting pot I referred to earlier. The organization I'm arguing for respects differences rather than seeking to smooth them out. It is multicultural rather than culture blind, which has an important consequence: When we no longer force people to "belong" to a common ethnicity or culture, then the organization's leaders must work all the harder to define belonging in terms of a set of values and a sense of purpose that transcend the interests, desires, and preferences of any one group.

6. *Modify Your Systems.* The first purpose of examining and modifying assumptions is to modify systems. Promotion, mentoring, and sponsorship comprise one

such system, and the unexamined cream-to-the-top assumption I mentioned earlier can tend to keep minorities and women from climbing the corporate ladder. After all, in many companies it is difficult to secure a promotion above a certain level without a personal advocate or sponsor. In the context of managing diversity, the question is not whether this system is maximally efficient but whether it works for all employees. Executives who only sponsor people like themselves are not making much of a contribution to the cause of getting the best from every employee.

Performance appraisal is another system where unexamined practices and patterns can have pernicious effects. For example, there are companies where official performance appraisals differ substantially from what is said informally, with the result that employees get their most accurate performance feedback through the grapevine. So if the grapevine is closed to minorities and women, they are left at a severe disadvantage. As one white manager observed, "If the blacks around here knew how they were really perceived, there would be a revolt." Maybe so. More important to your business, however, is the fact that without an accurate appraisal of performance, minority and women employees will find it difficult to correct or defend their alleged shortcomings.

7. *Modify Your Models.* The second purpose of modifying assumptions is to modify models of managerial and employee behavior. My own personal hobgoblin is one I call the Doer Model, often an outgrowth of the family assumption and of unchallenged paternalism.

Managers who get in the trenches with their workers are sometimes only looking for a place to hide.

I have found the Doer Model alive and thriving in a dozen companies. It works like this:

Since father knows best, managers seek subordinates who will follow their lead and do as they do. If they can't find people exactly like themselves, they try to find people who aspire to be exactly like themselves. The goal is predictability and immediate responsiveness because the doer manager is not there to manage people but to do the business. In accounting departments, for example, doer managers do accounting, and subordinates are simply extensions of their hands and minds, sensitive to every signal and suggestion of managerial intent.

Doer managers take pride in this identity of purpose. "I wouldn't ask my people to do anything I wouldn't do myself," they say. "I roll up my sleeves and get in the trenches." Doer managers love to be in the trenches. It keeps them out of the line of fire.

But managers aren't supposed to be in the trenches, and accounting managers aren't supposed to do accounting. What they are supposed to do is create systems and a climate that allow accountants to do accounting, a climate that enables people to do what they've been charged to do. The right goal is doer subordinates, supported and empowered by managers who manage.

8. *Help Your People Pioneer.* Learning to manage diversity is a change process, and the managers involved are change agents. There is no single tried and tested "solution" to diversity and no fixed right way to manage it. Assuming the existence of a single or even a dominant barrier undervalues the importance of all the other barriers that face any company, including, potentially, prejudice, personality, community dynamics, culture, and the ups and downs of business itself.

While top executives articulate the new company policy and their commitment to it, middle managers—most or all of them still white males, remember—are placed in the tough position of having to cope with a forest of problems and simultaneously develop the minorities and women who represent their own competition for an increasingly limited number of promotions. What's more, every time they stumble they will themselves be labeled the major barriers to progress. These managers need help, they need a certain amount of sympathy, and, most of all, perhaps, they need to be told that they are pioneers and judged accordingly.

In one case, an ambitious young black woman was assigned to a white male manager, at his request, on the basis of her excellent company record. They looked forward to working together, and for the first three months, everything went well. But then their relationship began to deteriorate, and the harder they worked at patching it up, the worse it got. Both of them, along with their superiors, were surprised by the conflict and seemed puzzled as to its causes. Eventually, the black woman requested and obtained reassignment. But even though they escaped each other, both suffered a sense of failure severe enough to threaten their careers.

What could have been done to assist them? Well, empathy would not have hurt. But perspective would have been better yet. In their particular company and situation, these two people had placed themselves at the cutting edge of race and gender relations. They needed to know that mistakes at the cutting edge are different—and potentially more valuable— than mistakes elsewhere.

Does this program or policy give special consideration to one group? If so, it won't solve your problem— and may have caused it.

Maybe they needed some kind of pioneer training. But at the very least they needed to be told that they were pioneers, that conflicts and failures came with the territory, and that they would be judged accordingly.

9. *Apply the Special Consideration Test.* I said earlier that affirmative action was an artificial, transitional, but necessary stage on the road to a truly diverse work force. Because of its artificial nature, affirmative action requires constant attention and drive to make it work. The point of learning once and for all how to manage diversity is that all that energy can be focused somewhere else.

There is a simple test to help you spot the diversity programs that are going to eat up enormous quantities of time and effort. Surprisingly, perhaps, it is the same test you might use to identify the programs and policies that created your problem in the first place. The test consists of one question: Does this program, policy, or principle give special consideration to one group? Will it contribute to everyone's success, or will it only produce an advantage for blacks or whites or women or men? Is it designed for *them* as opposed to *us*? Whenever the answer is yes, you're not yet on the road to managing diversity.

This does not rule out the possibility of addressing issues that relate to a single group. It only underlines the importance of determining that the issue you're addressing does not relate to other groups as well. For example, management in one company noticed that blacks were not moving up in the organization. Before instituting a special program to bring them along, managers conducted interviews to see if they could find the reason for the impasse. What blacks themselves reported was a problem with the quality of supervision. Further interviews showed that other employees too—including white males—were concerned about the quality of supervision and felt that little was being done to foster professional development. Correcting the situation eliminated a problem that affected everyone. In this case, a solution that focused only on blacks would have been out of place.

Had the problem consisted of prejudice, on the other hand, or some other barrier to blacks or minorities alone, a solution based on affirmative action would have been perfectly appropriate.

10. *Continue Affirmative Action.* Let me come full circle. The ability to manage diversity is the ability to manage your company without unnatural advantage or disadvantage for any member of your diverse work force. The fact remains that you must first have a work force that is diverse at every level, and if you don't, you're going to need affirmative action to get from here to there.

The reason you then want to move beyond affirmative action to managing diversity is because affirmative action fails to deal with the root causes of prejudice and inequality and does little to develop the full potential of every man and woman in the company. In a country seeking competitive advantage in a global economy, the goal of managing diversity is to develop our capacity to accept, incorporate, and empower the diverse human talents of the most diverse nation on earth. It's our reality. We need to make it our strength.

Out of the Numbers Game and into Decision Making

LIKE MANY OTHER COMPANIES, Avon practiced affirmative action in the 1970s and was not pleased with the results. The company worked with employment agencies that specialized in finding qualified minority hires, and it cultivated contacts with black and minority organizations on college campuses. Avon wanted to see its customer base reflected in its work force, especially at the decision-making level. But while women moved up the corporate ladder fairly briskly—not so surprising in a company whose work force is mostly female—minorities did not. So in 1984, the company began to change its policies and practices.

"We really wanted to get out of the numbers game," says Marcia Worthing, the corporate vice president for human resources. "We felt it was more important to have five minority people tied into the decision-making process than ten who were just heads to count."

First, Avon initiated awareness training at all levels. "The key to recruiting, retaining, and promoting minorities is not the human resource department," says Worthing. "It's getting line management to buy into the idea. We had to do more than change behavior. We had to change attitudes."

Second, the company formed a Multicultural Participation Council that meets regularly to oversee the process of managing diversity. The group includes Avon's CEO and high-level employees from throughout the company.

Third, in conjunction with the American Institute for Managing Diversity, Avon developed a diversity training program. For several years, the company has sent racially and ethnically diverse groups of 25 managers at a time to Institute headquarters at Morehouse College in Atlanta, where they spend three weeks confronting their differences and learning to hear and avail themselves of viewpoints they initially disagreed with. "We came away disciples of diversity," says one company executive.

Fourth, the company helped three minority groups—blacks, Hispanics, and Asians—form networks that criss-crossed the corporation in all 50 states. Each network elects its own leaders and has an adviser from senior management. In addition, the networks have representatives on the Multicultural Participation Council, where they serve as a conduit for employee views on diversity issues facing management.

"It Simply Makes Good Business Sense."

CORNING CHARACTERIZES ITS 1970s affirmative action program as a form of legal compliance. The law dictated affirmative action and morality required it, so the company did its best to hire minorities and women.

The ensuing cycle was classic: recruitment, confidence, disappointment, embarrassment, crisis, more recruitment. Talented women and blacks joined the company only to plateau or resign. Few reached upper management levels, and no one could say exactly why.

Then James R. Houghton took over as CEO in 1983 and made the diverse work force one of Corning's three top priorities, alongside Total Quality and a higher return on equity. His logic was twofold:

First of all, the company had higher attrition rates for minorities and women than for white males, which meant that investments in training and development were being wasted. Second, he believed that the Corning work force should more closely mirror the Corning customer base.

In order to break the cycle of recruitment and subsequent frustration, the company established two quality improvement teams headed by senior executives, one for black progress and one for women's progress. Mandatory awareness training was introduced for some 7,000 salaried employees—a day and a half for gender awareness, two-and-a-half days for racial awareness. One goal of the training is to identify unconscious company values that work against minorities and women. For example, a number of awareness groups reached the conclusion that working late had so much symbolic value that managers tended to look more at the quantity than at the quality of time spent on the job, with predictably negative effects on employees with dependent-care responsibilities.

The company also made an effort to improve communications by printing regular stories and articles about the diverse work force in its in-house newspaper and by publicizing employee success stories that emphasize diversity. It worked hard to identify and publicize promotion criteria. Career planning systems were introduced for all employees.

With regard to recruitment, Corning set up a nationwide scholarship program that provides renewable grants of $5,000 per year of college in exchange for a summer of paid work at some Corning installation. A majority of program participants have come to work for Corning full-time after graduation, and very few have left the company so far, though the program has been in place only four years.

The company also expanded its summer intern program, with an emphasis on minorities and women, and established formal recruiting contacts with campus groups like the Society of Women Engineers and the National Black MBA Association.

Corning sees its efforts to manage diversity not only as a social and moral issue but also as a question of efficiency and competitiveness. In the words of Mr. Houghton, "It simply makes good business sense."

Turning Social Pressures into Competitive Advantage

LIKE MOST OTHER COMPANIES trying to respond to the federal legislation of the 1970s, Digital started off by focusing on numbers. By the early 1980s, however, company leaders could see it would take more than recruitment to make Digital the diverse workplace they wanted it to be. Equal Employment Opportunity (EEO) and affirmative action seemed too exclusive—too much "white males doing good deeds for minorities and women." The company wanted to move beyond these programs to the kind of environment where every employee could realize his or her potential, and Digital decided that meant an environment where individual differences were not tolerated but valued, even celebrated.

The resulting program and philosophy, called Valuing Differences, has two components:

First, the company helps people get in touch with their stereotypes and false assumptions through what Digital calls Core Groups. These voluntary groupings of eight to ten people work with company-trained facilitators whose job is to encourage discussion and self-development and, in the company's words, "to keep people safe" as they struggle with their prejudices. Digital also runs a voluntary two-day training program called "Understanding the Dynamics of Diversity," which thousands of Digital employees have now taken.

Second, the company has named a number of senior managers to various Cultural Boards of Directors and

Valuing Differences Boards of Directors. These bodies promote openness to individual differences, encourage younger managers committed to the goal of diversity, and sponsor frequent celebrations of racial, gender, and ethnic differences such as Hispanic Heritage Week and Black History Month.

In addition to the Valuing Differences program, the company preserved its EEO and affirmative action functions. Valuing Differences focuses on personal and group development, EEO on legal issues, and affirmative action on systemic change. According to Alan Zimmerle, head of the Valuing Differences program, EEO and Valuing Differences are like two circles that touch but don't overlap—the first representing the legal need for diversity, the second the corporate desire for diversity. Affirmative action is a third circle that overlaps the other two and holds them together with policies and procedures.

Together, these three circles can transform legal and social pressures into the competitive advantage of a more effective work force, higher morale, and the reputation of being a better place to work. As Zimmerle puts it, "Digital wants to be the employer of choice. We want our pick of the talent that's out there."

Discovering Complexity and Value in P&G's Diversity

BECAUSE PROCTER & GAMBLE fills its upper level management positions only from within the company, it places a premium on recruiting the best available entry-level employees. Campus recruiting is pursued nationwide and year-round by line managers from all levels of the company. Among other things, the company has made a concerted—and successful—effort to find and hire talented minorities and women.

Finding first-rate hires is only one piece of the effort, however. There is still the challenge of moving diversity upward. As one top executive put it, "We know that we can only succeed as a company if we have an environment that makes it easy for all of us, not just some of us, to work to our potential."

In May 1988, P&G formed a Corporate Diversity Strategy Task Force to clarify the concept of diversity, define its importance for the company, and identify strategies for making progress toward successfully managing a diverse work force.

The task force, composed of men and women from every corner of the company, made two discoveries: First, diversity at P&G was far more complex than most people had supposed. In addition to race and gender, it included factors such as cultural heritage, personal background, and functional experience. Second, the company needed to expand its view of the value of differences.

The task force helped the company to see that learning to manage diversity would be a long-term process of organizational change. For example, P&G has offered voluntary diversity training at all levels since the 1970s, but the program has gradually broadened its emphasis on race and gender awareness to include the value of self-realization in a diverse environment. As retiring board chairman John Smale put it, "If we can tap the total contribution that everybody in our company has to offer, we will be better and more competitive in everything we do."

P&G is now conducting a thorough, continuing evaluation of all management programs to be sure that systems are working well for everyone. It has also carried out a corporate survey to get a better picture of the problems facing P&G employees who are balancing work and family responsibilities and to improve company programs in such areas as dependent care.

The Daily Experience of Genuine Workplace Diversity

CHAIRMAN DAVID T. KEARNS believes that a firm and resolute commitment to affirmative action is the first and most important step to work force diversity." Xerox is committed to affirmative action," he says. "It is a corporate value, a management priority, and a formal business objective."

Xerox began recruiting minorities and women systematically as far back as the mid-1960s, and it pioneered such concepts as pivotal jobs (described later). The company's approach emphasizes behavior expectations as opposed to formal consciousness-raising programs because, as one Xerox executive put it, "It's just not realistic to think that a day and a half of training will change a person's thinking after 30 or 40 years."

On the assumption that attitude changes will grow from the daily experience of genuine workplace diversity, the Xerox Balanced Work Force Strategy sets goals for the number of minorities and women in each division and at every level. (For example, the goal for the top 300 executive-level jobs in one large division is 35% women by 1995, compared with 15% today.) "You *must* have a laboratory to work in," says Ted Payne, head of Xerox's Office of Affirmative Action and Equal Opportunity.

Minority and women's employee support groups have grown up in more than a dozen locations with the company's encouragement. But Xerox depends mainly on the three pieces of its balanced strategy to make diversity work.

First are the goals. Xerox sets recruitment and representation goals in accordance with federal guidelines and reviews them constantly to make sure they reflect work force demographics. Any company with a federal contract is required to make this effort. But Xerox then extends the guidelines by setting diversity goals for its upper level jobs and holding division and group managers accountable for reaching them.

The second piece is a focus on pivotal jobs, a policy Xerox adopted in the 1970s when it first noticed that minorities and women did not have the upward mobility the company wanted to see. By examining the backgrounds of top executives, Xerox was able to identify the key positions that all successful managers had held at lower levels and to set goals for getting minorities and women assigned to such jobs.

The third piece is an effort to concentrate managerial training not so much on managing diversity as on just plain managing people. What the company discovered when it began looking at managerial behavior toward minorities and women was that all too many managers didn't know enough about how to manage anyone, let alone people quite different from themselves.

Originally published in March–April 1990
Reprint 90213

Making Differences Matter

A New Paradigm for Managing Diversity

DAVID A. THOMAS AND ROBIN J. ELY

Executive Summary

DIVERSITY EFFORTS IN the workplace have been under-taken with great goodwill, but, ironically, they often end up fueling tensions. They rarely spur the leaps in organizational effectiveness that are possible. Two paradigms for diversity are responsible, but a new one is showing it can address the problem.

The discrimination-and-fairness paradigm is based on the recognition that discrimination is wrong. Under it, progress is measured by how well the company achieves its recruitment and retention goals. The paradigm idealizes assimilation and color- and gender-blind conformism. The access-and-legitimacy paradigm, on the other hand, celebrates differences. Under it, organizations seek access to a more diverse clientele, matching their demographics to targeted consumers. But that paradigm can leave employees of different identity-group affiliations feeling marginalized or exploited.

In companies with the right kind of leadership, a third paradigm is showing that beneficial learning takes place and organizations become more effective in fulfilling their missions if employees are encouraged to tap their differences for creative ideas. If all or most of eight preconditions are in place, the opportunities for growth are almost unlimited.

Leaders in third-paradigm companies are proactive about learning from diversity; they encourage people to make explicit use of cultural experience at work; they fight all forms of dominance and subordination, including those generated by one functional group acting superior to another; and they ensure that the inevitable tensions that come from a genuine effort to make way for diversity are acknowledged and resolved with sensitivity.

Why should companies concern themselves with diversity? Until recently, many managers answered this question with the assertion that discrimination is wrong, both legally and morally. But today managers are voicing a second notion as well. A more diverse workforce, they say, will increase organizational effectiveness. It will lift morale, bring greater access to new segments of the marketplace, and enhance productivity. In short, they claim, diversity will be good for business.

Yet if this is true—and we believe it is—where are the positive impacts of diversity? Numerous and varied initiatives to increase diversity in corporate America have been under way for more than two decades. Rarely, however, have those efforts spurred leaps in organizational effectiveness. Instead, many attempts to increase diversity in the workplace have backfired, sometimes even heightening tensions among employees and hindering a company's performance.

This article offers an explanation for why diversity efforts are not fulfilling their promise and presents a new paradigm for understanding—and leveraging—diversity. It is our belief that there is a distinct way to unleash the powerful benefits of a diverse workforce. Although these benefits include increased profitability, they go beyond financial measures to encompass learning, creativity, flexibility, organizational and individual growth, and the ability of a company to adjust rapidly and successfully to market changes. The desired transformation, however, requires a fundamental change in the attitudes and behaviors of an organization's leadership. And that will come only when senior managers abandon an underlying and flawed assumption about diversity and replace it with a broader understanding.

Most people assume that workplace diversity is about increasing racial, national, gender, or class representation—in other words, recruiting and retaining more people from traditionally underrepresented "identity groups." Taking this commonly held assumption as a starting point, we set out six years ago to investigate its link to organizational effectiveness. We soon found that thinking of diversity simply in terms of identity-group representation inhibited effectiveness.

The new understanding of diversity involves more than increasing the number of different identity groups on the payroll.

Organizations usually take one of two paths in managing diversity. In the name of equality and fairness, they encourage (and expect) women and people of color to blend in. Or they set them apart in jobs that relate specifically to their backgrounds, assigning them, for example, to areas that require them to interface with clients or customers of the same identity group. African American M.B.A.'s often find themselves marketing products to inner-city communities; Hispanics frequently market to Hispanics or work for Latin American subsidiaries. In those kinds of cases, companies are operating on the assumption that the main virtue identity groups have to offer is a knowledge of their own people. This assumption is limited—and limiting—and detrimental to diversity efforts.

What we suggest here is that diversity goes beyond increasing the number of different identity-group affiliations on the payroll to recognizing that such an effort is merely the first step in managing a diverse workforce for the organization's utmost benefit. Diversity should be understood as *the varied perspectives and approaches to work* that members of different identity groups bring.

Women, Hispanics, Asian Americans, African Americans, Native Americans—these groups and others outside the mainstream of corporate America don't bring with them just their "insider information." They bring different, important, and competitively relevant knowledge and perspectives about how to actually *do work*— how to design processes, reach goals, frame tasks, create effective teams, communicate ideas, and lead. When allowed to, members of these groups can help companies grow and improve by challenging basic assumptions about an organization's functions, strategies, operations, practices, and procedures. And in doing so, they are able to bring more of their whole selves to the workplace and identify more fully with the work they do, setting in motion a virtuous circle. Certainly, individuals can be expected to contribute to a company their firsthand familiarity with niche markets. But only when companies start thinking about diversity more holistically—as providing fresh and meaningful approaches to work—and stop assuming that diversity relates simply to how a person looks or where he or she comes from, will they be able to reap its full rewards.

Two perspectives have guided most diversity initiatives to date: the *discrimination-and-fairness paradigm* and the *access-and-legitimacy paradigm*. But we have identified a new, emerging approach to this complex management issue. This approach, which we call the *learning-and-effectiveness paradigm*, incorporates aspects of the first two paradigms but goes beyond them by concretely connecting diversity to approaches to work. Our goal is to help business leaders see what their own approach to diversity currently is and how it may already have influenced their companies' diversity efforts. Managers can learn to assess whether they need to change their diversity initiatives and, if so, how to accomplish that change.

The following discussion will also cite several examples of how connecting the new definition of diversity to the actual *doing* of work has led some organizations to markedly better performance. The organizations differ in many ways—none are in the same industry, for instance—but they are united by one similarity: Their leaders realize that increasing demographic variation does not in itself increase organizational effectiveness. They realize that it is *how* a company defines diversity—

and *what it does* with the experiences of being a diverse organization—that delivers on the promise.

The Discrimination-and-Fairness Paradigm

Using the discrimination-and-fairness paradigm is perhaps thus far the dominant way of understanding diversity. Leaders who look at diversity through this lens usually focus on equal opportunity, fair treatment, recruitment, and compliance with federal Equal Employment Opportunity requirements. The paradigm's underlying logic can be expressed as follows:

> *Prejudice has kept members of certain demographic groups out of organizations such as ours. As a matter of fairness and to comply with federal mandates, we need to work toward restructuring the makeup of our organization to let it more closely reflect that of society. We need managerial processes that ensure that all our employees are treated equally and with respect and that some are not given unfair advantage over others.*

Although it resembles the thinking behind traditional affirmative-action efforts, the discrimination-and-fairness paradigm does go beyond a simple concern with numbers. Companies that operate with this philosophical orientation often institute mentoring and career-development programs specifically for the women and people of color in their ranks and train other employees to respect cultural differences. Under this paradigm, nevertheless, progress in diversity is measured by how well the company achieves its recruitment and retention goals rather than by the degree to which conditions in the company allow employees to draw on their personal assets and perspectives to do their work more effectively.

The staff, one might say, gets diversified, but the work does not.

What are some of the common characteristics of companies that have used the discrimination-and-fairness paradigm successfully to increase their demographic diversity? Our research indicates that they are usually run by leaders who value due process and equal treatment of all employees and who have the authority to use top-down directives to enforce initiatives based on those attitudes. Such companies are often bureaucratic in structure, with control processes in place for monitoring, measuring, and rewarding individual performance. And finally, they are often organizations with entrenched, easily observable cultures, in which values like fairness are widespread and deeply inculcated and codes of conduct are clear and unambiguous. (Perhaps the most extreme example of an organization in which all these factors are at work is the United States Army.)

Without doubt, there are benefits to this paradigm: it does tend to increase demographic diversity in an organization, and it often succeeds in promoting fair treatment. But it also has significant limitations. The first of these is that its color-blind, gender-blind ideal is to some degree built on the implicit assumption that "we are all the same" or "we aspire to being all the same." Under this paradigm, it is not desirable for diversification of the workforce to influence the organization's work or culture. The company should operate as if every person were of the same race, gender, and nationality. It is unlikely that leaders who manage

Companies need open and explicit discussion of how differences can be used as sources of individual and organizational effectiveness.

diversity under this paradigm will explore how people's differences generate a potential diversity of effective ways of working, leading, viewing the market, managing people, and learning.

Not only does the discrimination-and-fairness paradigm insist that everyone is the same, but, with its emphasis on equal treatment, it puts pressure on employees to make sure that important differences among them do not count. Genuine disagreements about work definition, therefore, are sometimes wrongly interpreted through this paradigm's fairness-unfairness lens—especially when honest disagreements are accompanied by tense debate. A female employee who insists, for example, that a company's advertising strategy is not appropriate for all ethnic segments in the marketplace might feel she is violating the code of assimilation upon which the paradigm is built. Moreover, if she were then to defend her opinion by citing, let us say, her personal knowledge of the ethnic group the company wanted to reach, she might risk being perceived as importing inappropriate attitudes into an organization that prides itself on being blind to cultural differences.

Workplace paradigms channel organizational thinking in powerful ways. By limiting the ability of employees to acknowledge openly their work-related but culturally based differences, the paradigm actually undermines the organization's capacity to learn about and improve its own strategies, processes, and practices. And it also keeps people from identifying strongly and personally with their work—a critical source of motivation and self-regulation in any business environment.

As an illustration of the paradigm's weaknesses, consider the case of Iversen Dunham, an international consulting firm that focuses on foreign and domestic economic-development policy. (Like all the examples in this article, the company is real, but its name is disguised.) Not long ago, the firm's managers asked us to help them understand why race relations had become a divisive issue precisely at a time when Iversen was receiving accolades for its diversity efforts. Indeed, other organizations had even begun to use the firm to benchmark their own diversity programs.

Iversen's diversity efforts had begun in the early 1970s, when senior managers decided to pursue greater racial and gender diversity in the firm's higher ranks. (The firm's leaders were strongly committed to the cause of social justice.) Women and people of color were hired and charted on career paths toward becoming project leaders. High performers among those who had left the firm were persuaded to return in senior roles. By 1989, about 50% of Iversen's project leaders and professionals were women, and 30% were people of color. The 13-member management committee, once exclusively white and male, included five women and four people of color. Additionally, Iversen had developed a strong contingent of foreign nationals.

It was at about this time, however, that tensions began to surface. Senior managers found it hard to believe that, after all the effort to create a fair and mutually respectful work community, some staff members could still be claiming that Iversen had racial discrimination problems. The management invited us to study the firm and deliver an outsider's assessment of its problem.

We had been inside the firm for only a short time when it became clear that Iversen's leaders viewed the dynamics of diversity through the lens of the discrimination-and-fairness paradigm. But where they saw racial discord, we discerned clashing approaches to the actual work of consulting. Why? Our research showed that tensions were strongest among midlevel project leaders. Surveys and interviews indicated that white project leaders welcomed demographic diversity as a general sign of progress but that they also thought the new employees were somehow changing the company, pulling it away from its original culture and its mission. Common criticisms were that African American and Hispanic staff made problems too complex by linking issues the organization had traditionally regarded as unrelated and that they brought on projects that seemed to require greater cultural sensitivity. White male project leaders also complained that their peers who were women and people of color were undermining one of Iversen's traditional strengths: its hard-core quantitative orientation. For instance, minority project leaders had suggested that Iversen consultants collect information and seek input from others in the client company besides senior managers—that is, from the rank and file and from middle managers. Some had urged Iversen to expand its consulting approach to include the gathering and analysis of qualitative data through interviewing and observation. Indeed, these project leaders had even challenged one of Iversen's long-standing, core assumptions: that the firm's reports were objective. They urged Iversen Dunham to recognize and address the subjective aspect of its analyses; the firm could, for example, include in its reports to clients dissenting Iversen views, if any existed.

For their part, project leaders who were women and people of color felt that they were not accorded the same level of authority to carry out that work as their white male peers. Moreover, they sensed that those peers were skeptical of their opinions, and they resented that doubts were not voiced openly.

Meanwhile, there also was some concern expressed about tension between white managers and nonwhite subordinates, who claimed they were being treated unfairly. But our analysis suggested that the manager-subordinate conflicts were not numerous enough to warrant the attention they were drawing from top management. We believed it was significant that senior managers found it easier to focus on this second type of conflict than on mid-level conflicts about project choice and project definition. Indeed, Iversen Dunham's focus seemed to be a result of the firm's reliance on its particular diversity paradigm and the emphasis on fairness and equality. It was relatively easy to diagnose problems in light of those concepts and to devise a solution: just get managers to treat their subordinates more fairly.

In contrast, it was difficult to diagnose peer-to-peer tensions in the framework of this model. Such conflicts were about the very nature of Iversen's work, not simply unfair treatment. Yes, they were related to identity-group affiliations, but they were not symptomatic of classic racism. It was Iversen's paradigm that led managers to interpret them as such. Remember, we were asked to assess what was supposed to be a racial discrimination problem. Iversen's discrimination-and-fairness paradigm had created a kind of cognitive blind spot; and, as a result, the company's leadership could not frame the problem accurately or solve it effectively. Instead, the company needed a cultural shift—it needed to grasp what to do with its diversity once it had achieved the numbers. If all Iversen Dunham employees were to contribute to the fullest extent, the company would need a paradigm that would encourage open and explicit discussion of what identity-group differences really mean and how they can be used as sources of individual and organizational effectiveness.

Today, mainly because of senior managers' resistance to such a cultural transformation, Iversen continues to struggle with the tensions arising from the diversity of its workforce.

The Access-and-Legitimacy Paradigm

In the competitive climate of the 1980s and 1990s, a new rhetoric and rationale for managing diversity emerged. If the discrimination-and-fairness paradigm can be said to have idealized assimilation and color- and gender-blind conformism, the access-and-legitimacy paradigm was predicated on the acceptance and celebration of differences. The underlying motivation of the access-and-legitimacy paradigm can be expressed this way:

> *We are living in an increasingly multicultural country, and new ethnic groups are quickly gaining consumer power. Our company needs a demographically more diverse workforce to help us gain access to these differentiated segments. We need employees with multilingual skills in order to understand and serve our customers better and to gain legitimacy with them. Diversity isn't just fair; it makes business sense.*

Where this paradigm has taken hold, organizations have pushed for access to—and legitimacy with—a more diverse clientele by matching the demographics of the organization to those of critical consumer or constituent groups. In some cases, the effort has led to substantial increases in organizational diversity. In investment banks, for example, municipal finance departments have long led corporate finance departments in pursuing demographic diversity because of the typical makeup of the administration of city halls and county boards. Many consumer-products companies that have used market segmentation based on gender, racial, and other demographic differences have also frequently created dedicated marketing positions for each segment. The paradigm has therefore led to new professional and managerial opportunities for women and people of color.

What are the common characteristics of organizations that have successfully used the access-and-legitimacy paradigm to increase their demographic diversity? There is but one: such companies almost always operate in a business environment in which there is increased diversity among customers, clients, or the labor pool—and therefore a clear opportunity or an imminent threat to the company.

Again, the paradigm has its strengths. Its market-based motivation and the potential for competitive advantage that it suggests are often qualities an entire company can understand and therefore support. But the paradigm is perhaps more notable for its limitations. In their pursuit of niche markets, access-and-legitimacy organizations tend to emphasize the role of cultural differences in a company without really analyzing those differences to see how they actually affect the work that is done. Whereas discrimination-and-fairness leaders are too quick to subvert differences in the interest of preserving harmony, access-and-legitimacy leaders are too quick to push staff with niche capabilities into differentiated pigeonholes without trying to understand what those capabilities really are and how they could be integrated into the company's mainstream work. To illustrate our point, we present the case of Access Capital.

Access Capital International is a U.S. investment bank that in the early 1980s launched an aggressive plan to expand into Europe. Initially, however, Access encountered serious problems opening offices in international markets; the people from the United States who were installed abroad lacked credibility, were ignorant of local cultural norms and market conditions, and simply couldn't seem to connect with native clients. Access responded by hiring Europeans who had attended North American business schools and by assigning them in teams to the foreign offices. This strategy was a marked success. Before long, the leaders of Access could take enormous pride in the fact that their European operations were highly profitable and staffed by a truly international corps of professionals. They took to calling the company "the best investment bank in the world."

Several years passed. Access's foreign offices continued to thrive, but some leaders were beginning to sense that the company was not fully benefiting from its diversity efforts. Indeed, some even suspected that the bank had made itself vulnerable because of how it had chosen to manage diversity. A senior executive from the United States explains:

> *If the French team all resigned tomorrow, what would we do? I'm not sure what we could do! We've never attempted to learn what these differences and cultural competencies really are, how they change the process of doing business. What is the German country team actually doing? We don't know. We know they're good, but we don't know the subtleties of how they do what they do. We assumed—and I think correctly—that culture makes a difference, but that's about as far as we went. We hired Europeans with American M.B.A.'s because we didn't know why we couldn't do business in Europe—we just*

assumed there was something cultural about why we couldn't connect. And ten years later, we still don't know what it is. If we knew, then perhaps we could take it and teach it. Which part of the investment banking process is universal and which part of it draws upon particular cultural competencies? What are the commonalities and differences? I may not be German, but maybe I could do better at understanding what it means to be an American doing business in Germany. Our company's biggest failing is that the department heads in London and the directors of the various country teams have never talked about these cultural identity issues openly. We knew enough to use people's cultural strengths, as it were, but we never seemed to learn from them.

Access's story makes an important point about the main limitation of the access-and-legitimacy paradigm: under its influence, the motivation for diversity usually emerges from very immediate and often crisis-oriented needs for access and legitimacy—in this case, the need to broker deals in European markets. However, once the organization appears to be achieving its goal, the leaders seldom go on to identify and analyze the culturally based skills, beliefs, and practices that worked so well. Nor do they consider how the organization can incorporate and learn from those skills, beliefs, or practices in order to capitalize on diversity in the long run.

When a business regards employees' experience as useful only to gain access to narrow markets, those employees may feel exploited.

Under the access-and-legitimacy paradigm, it was as if the bank's country teams had become little spin-off companies in their own right, doing their own exotic,

slightly mysterious cultural-diversity thing in a niche
market of their own, using competencies that for some
reason could not become more fully integrated into the
larger organization's understanding of itself. Difference
was valued within Access Capital—hence the development of country teams in the first place—but not valued
enough that the organization would try to integrate it
into the very core of its culture and into its business
practices.

Finally, the access-and-legitimacy paradigm can leave
some employees feeling exploited. Many organizations
using this paradigm have diversified only in those areas
in which they interact with particular niche-market segments. In time, many individuals recruited for this function have come to feel devalued and used as they begin
to sense that opportunities in other parts of the organization are closed to them. Often the larger organization
regards the experience of these employees as more limited or specialized, even though many of them in fact
started their careers in the mainstream market before
moving to special markets where their cultural backgrounds were a recognized asset. Also, many of these
people say that when companies have needed to down-
size or narrow their marketing focus, it is the special
departments that are often the first to go. That situation
creates tenuous and ultimately untenable career paths
for employees in the special departments.

The Emerging Paradigm: Connecting Diversity to Work Perspectives

Recently, in the course of our research, we have encountered a small number of organizations that, having relied
initially on one of the above paradigms to guide their

diversity efforts, have come to believe that they are not making the most of their own pluralism. These organizations, like Access Capital, recognize that employees frequently make decisions and choices at work that draw upon their cultural background—choices made because of their identity-group affiliations. The companies have also developed an outlook on diversity that enables them to *incorporate* employees' perspectives into the main work of the organization and to enhance work by rethinking primary tasks and redefining markets, products, strategies, missions, business practices, and even cultures. Such companies are using the learning-and-effectiveness paradigm for managing diversity and, by doing so, are tapping diversity's true benefits.

A case in point is Dewey & Levin, a small public-interest law firm located in a northeastern U.S. city. Although Dewey & Levin had long been a profitable practice, by the mid-1980s its all-white legal staff had become concerned that the women they represented in employment-related disputes were exclusively white. The firm's attorneys viewed that fact as a deficiency in light of their mandate to advocate on behalf of all women. Using the thinking behind the access-and-legitimacy paradigm, they also saw it as bad for business.

Shortly thereafter, the firm hired a Hispanic female attorney. The partners' hope, simply put, was that she would bring in clients from her own community and also demonstrate the firm's commitment to representing all women. But something even bigger than that happened. The new attorney introduced ideas to Dewey & Levin about what kinds of cases it should take on. Senior managers were open to those ideas and pursued them with great success. More women of color were hired, and they, too, brought fresh perspectives. The firm now pursues cases that its previously all-white legal staff would not have thought relevant or appropriate because the link between the firm's mission and the employment issues involved in the cases would not have been obvious to them. For example, the firm has pursued precedent-setting litigation that challenges English-only policies—an area that it once would have ignored because such policies did not fall under the purview of traditional affirmative-action work. Yet it now sees a link between English-only policies and employment issues for a large group of women—primarily recent immigrants—whom it had previously failed to serve adequately. As one of the white principals explains, the demographic composition of Dewey & Levin "has affected the work in terms of expanding notions of what are [relevant] issues and taking on issues and framing them in creative ways that would have never been done [with an all-white staff]. It's really changed the substance—and in that sense enhanced the quality—of our work."

Dewey & Levin's increased business success has reinforced its commitment to diversity. In addition, people of color at the firm uniformly report feeling respected, not simply "brought along as window dressing." Many of the new attorneys say their perspectives are heard with a kind of openness and interest they have never experienced before in a work setting. Not surprisingly, the firm has had little difficulty attracting and retaining a competent and diverse professional staff.

If the discrimination-and-fairness paradigm is organized around the theme of assimilation—in which the aim is to achieve a demographically representative workforce whose members treat one another exactly the same—then the access-and-legitimacy paradigm can be regarded as coalescing around an almost opposite concept: differentiation, in which the objective is to place different people where their demographic characteristics match those of important constituents and markets.

The emerging paradigm, in contrast to both, organizes itself around the overarching theme of integration. Assimilation goes too far in pursuing sameness. Differentiation, as we have shown, overshoots in the other direction. The new model for managing diversity transcends both. Like the fairness paradigm, it promotes equal opportunity for all individuals. And like the access paradigm, it acknowledges cultural differences among people and recognizes the value in those differences. Yet this new model for managing diversity lets the organization internalize differences among employees so that it learns and grows because of them. Indeed, with the model fully in place, members of the organization can say, We are all on the same team, *with* our differences— not *despite* them.

Eight Preconditions for Making the Paradigm Shift

Dewey & Levin may be atypical in its eagerness to open itself up to change and engage in a long-term transformation process. We remain convinced, however, that unless organizations that are currently in the grip of the other two paradigms can revise their view of diversity so as to avoid cognitive blind spots, opportunities will be missed, tensions will most likely be misdiagnosed, and companies will continue to find the potential benefits of diversity elusive.

Hence the question arises: What is it about the law firm of Dewey & Levin and other emerging third-paradigm companies that enables them to make the most of their diversity? Our research suggests that there are eight preconditions that help to position organizations to use identity-group differences in the service of organizational learning, growth, and renewal.

1. **The leadership must understand that a diverse workforce will embody different perspectives and approaches to work, and must truly value variety of opinion and insight.** We know of a financial services company that once assumed that the only successful sales model was one that utilized aggressive, rapid-fire cold calls. (Indeed, its incentive system rewarded salespeople in large part for the number of calls made.) An internal review of the company's diversity initiatives, however, showed that the company's first- and third-most-profitable employees were women who were most likely to use a sales technique based on the slow but sure building of relationships. The company's top management has now made the link between different identity groups and different approaches to how work gets done and has come to see that there is more than one right way to get positive results.

2. **The leadership must recognize both the learning opportunities and the challenges that the expression of different perspectives presents for an organization.** In other words, the second precondition is a leadership that is committed to persevering during the long process of learning and relearning that the new paradigm requires.

3. **The organizational culture must create an expectation of high standards of performance from everyone.** Such a culture isn't one that expects less from some employees than from others. Some orga-

nizations expect women and people of color to underperform—a negative assumption that too often becomes a self-fulfilling prophecy. To move to the third paradigm, a company must believe that all its members can and should contribute fully.

4. **The organizational culture must stimulate personal development.** Such a culture brings out people's full range of useful knowledge and skills—usually through the careful design of jobs that allow people to grow and develop but also through training and education programs.

5. **The organizational culture must encourage openness.** Such a culture instills a high tolerance for debate and supports constructive conflict on work-related matters.

6. **The culture must make workers feel valued.** If this precondition is met, workers feel committed to—and empowered within—the organization and therefore feel comfortable taking the initiative to apply their skills and experiences in new ways to enhance their job performance.

7. **The organization must have a well-articulated and widely understood mission.** Such a mission enables people to be clear about what the company is trying to accomplish. It grounds and guides discussions about work-related changes that staff members might sug-

Leaders who appreciate differences fight all forms of dominance, including any functional area's presumption of superiority over another.

gest. Being clear about the company's mission helps keep discussions about work differences from degenerating into debates about the validity of people's perspectives. A clear mission provides a focal point that keeps the discussion centered on accomplishment of goals.

8. **The organization must have a relatively egalitarian, nonbureaucratic structure.** It's important to have a structure that promotes the exchange of ideas and welcomes constructive challenges to the usual way of doing things—from any employee with valuable experience. Forward-thinking leaders in bureaucratic organizations must retain the organization's efficiency-promoting control systems and chains of command while finding ways to reshape the change-resisting mind-set of the classic bureaucratic model. They need to separate the enabling elements of bureaucracy (the ability to get things done) from the disabling elements of bureaucracy (those that create resistance to experimentation).

First Interstate Bank: A Paradigm Shift in Progress

All eight preconditions do not have to be in place in order to begin a shift from the first or second diversity orientations toward the learning-and-effectiveness paradigm. But most should be. First Interstate Bank, a midsize bank operating in a midwestern city, illustrates this point.

First Interstate, admittedly, is not a typical bank. Its client base is a minority community, and its mission is expressly to serve that base through "the development of a highly talented workforce." The bank is unique in other ways: its leadership welcomes constructive criticism; its structure is relatively egalitarian and nonbureaucratic; and its culture is open-minded. Nevertheless, First Interstate had long enforced a policy that loan officers had to hold college degrees. Those without were hired only for support-staff jobs and were never promoted beyond or outside support functions.

Two years ago, however, the support staff began to challenge the policy. Many of them had been with First Interstate for many years and, with the company's active support, had improved their skills through training. Others had expanded their skills on the job, again with the bank's encouragement, learning to run credit checks, prepare presentations for clients, and even calculate the algorithms necessary for many loan decisions. As a result, some people on the support staff were doing many of the same tasks as loan officers. Why, then, they wondered, couldn't they receive commensurate rewards in title and compensation?

This questioning led to a series of contentious meetings between the support staff and the bank's senior managers. It soon became clear that the problem called for managing diversity—diversity based not on race or gender but on class. The support personnel were uniformly from lower socioeconomic communities than were the college-educated loan officers. Regardless, the principle was the same as for race- or gender-based diversity problems. The support staff had different ideas about how the work of the bank should be done. They argued that those among them with the requisite skills should be allowed to rise through the ranks to professional positions, and they believed their ideas were not being heard or accepted.

Their beliefs challenged assumptions that the company's leadership had long held about which employees should have the authority to deal with customers and about how much responsibility administrative employees should ultimately receive. In order to take up this challenge, the bank would have to be open to exploring the requirements that a new perspective would impose on it. It would need to consider the possibility of mapping out an educational and career path for people without degrees—a path that could put such workers on the road to becoming loan officers. In other words, the leadership would have to transform itself willingly and embrace fluidity in policies that in times past had been clearly stated and unquestioningly held.

Today the bank's leadership is undergoing just such a transformation. The going, however, is far from easy. The bank's senior managers now must look beyond the tensions and acrimony sparked by the debate over differing work perspectives and consider the bank's new direction an important learning and growth opportunity.

Shift Complete: Third-Paradigm Companies in Action

First Interstate is a shift in progress; but, in addition to Dewey & Levin, there are several organizations we know of for which the shift is complete. In these cases, company leaders have played a critical role as facilitators and tone setters. We have observed in particular that in organizations that have adopted the new perspective, leaders and managers—and, following in their tracks, employees in general—are taking four kinds of action.

They are making the mental connection. First, in organizations that have adopted the new perspective, the leaders are actively seeking opportunities to explore how identity-group differences affect relationships among workers and affect the way work gets done. They are investing considerable time and energy in understanding how identity-group memberships take on social meanings in the organization and how those meanings manifest themselves in the way work is defined, assigned, and accomplished. When there is no proactive search to understand, then learning from diversity, if it happens at all, can occur only reactively—that is, in response to diversity-related crises.

The situation at Iversen Dunham illustrates the missed opportunities resulting from that scenario. Rather than seeing differences in the way project leaders defined and approached their work as an opportunity to gain new insights and develop new approaches to achieving its mission, the firm remained entrenched in its traditional ways, able to arbitrate such differences only by thinking about what was fair and what was racist. With this quite limited view of the role race can play in an organization, discussions about the topic become fraught with fear and defensiveness, and everyone misses out on insights about how race might influence work in positive ways.

A second case, however, illustrates how some leaders using the new paradigm have been able to envision—and make—the connection between cultural diversity and the company's work. A vice president of Mastiff, a large national insurance company, received a complaint from one of the managers in her unit, an African American man. The manager wanted to demote an African American woman he had hired for a leadership position from another Mastiff division just three months before. He told the vice president he was profoundly disappointed with the performance of his new hire.

"I hired her because I was pretty certain she had tremendous leadership skill," he said. "I knew she had a management style that was very open and empowering. I was also sure she'd have a great impact on the rest of the management team. But she hasn't done any of that."

Surprised, the vice president tried to find out from him what he thought the problem was, but she was not getting any answers that she felt really defined or illuminated the root of the problem. Privately, it puzzled her that someone would decide to demote a 15-year veteran of the company—and a minority woman at that—so soon after bringing her to his unit.

The vice president probed further. In the course of the conversation, the manager happened to mention that he knew the new employee from church and was familiar with the way she handled leadership there and in other community settings. In those less formal situations, he had seen her perform as an extremely effective, sensitive, and influential leader.

That is when the vice president made an interpretive leap. "If that's what you know about her," the vice president said to the manager, "then the question for us is, why can't she bring those skills to work here?" The vice president decided to arrange a meeting with all three present to ask this very question directly. In the meeting, the African American woman explained, "I didn't think I would last long if I acted that way here. My personal style of leadership—that particular style—works well if you have the permission to do it fully; then you can just do it and not have to look over your shoulder."

Pointing to the manager who had planned to fire her, she added, "He's right. The style of leadership I use outside this company can definitely be effective. But I've been at Mastiff for 15 years. I know this organization, and I know if I brought that piece of myself—if I became that authentic—I just wouldn't survive here."

What this example illustrates is that the vice president's learning-and-effectiveness paradigm led her to explore and then make the link between cultural diversity and work style. What was occurring, she realized, was a mismatch between the cultural background of the recently promoted woman and the cultural environment of her work setting. It had little to do with private attitudes or feelings, or gender issues, or some inherent lack of leadership ability. The source of the underperformance was that the newly promoted woman had a certain style and the organization's culture did not support her in expressing it comfortably. The vice president's paradigm led her to ask new questions and to seek out new information, but, more important, it also led her to interpret existing information differently.

The two senior managers began to realize that part of the African American woman's inability to see herself as a leader at work was that she had for so long been undervalued in the organization. And, in a sense, she had become used to splitting herself off from who she was in her own community. In the 15 years she had been at Mastiff, she had done her job well as an individual contributor, but she had never received any signals that her bosses wanted her to draw on her cultural competencies in order to lead effectively.

They are legitimating open discussion. Leaders and managers who have adopted the new paradigm are taking the initiative to "green light" open discussion about how identity-group memberships inform and influence an employee's experience and the organization's behavior. They are encouraging people to make *explicit* use of background cultural experience and the pools of knowledge gained outside the organization to inform and enhance their work. Individuals often do use their cultural competencies at work, but in a closeted, almost embarrassed, way. The unfortunate result is that the opportunity for collective and organizational learning and improvement is lost.

The case of a Chinese woman who worked as a chemist at Torinno Food Company illustrates this point. Linda was part of a product development group at Torinno when a problem arose with the flavoring of a new soup. After the group had made a number of scientific attempts to correct the problem, Linda came up with the solution by "setting aside my chemistry and drawing on my understanding of Chinese cooking." She did not, however, share with her colleagues—all of them white males—the real source of her inspiration for the solution for fear that it would set her apart or that they might consider her unprofessional. Overlaid on the cultural issue, of course, was a gender issue (women cooking) as well as a work-family issue (women doing *home* cooking in a chemistry lab). All of these themes had erected unspoken boundaries that Linda knew could be career-damaging for her to cross. After solving the problem, she simply went back to the so-called scientific way of doing things.

Senior managers at Torinno Foods in fact had made a substantial commitment to diversifying the workforce through a program designed to teach employees to value the contributions of all its members. Yet Linda's perceptions indicate that, in the actual day-to-day context of work, the program had failed—and in precisely one of those areas where it would have been important for it to have worked. It had failed to affirm someone's identity-group experiences as a legitimate source of insight into her work. It is likely that this organization will miss future opportunities to take full advantage of the talent of employees such as Linda. When people believe that they must suggest and apply their ideas covertly, the organization also misses opportunities to discuss, debate, refine, and build on those ideas fully. In addition, because individuals like Linda will continue to think that they must hide parts of themselves in order to fit in, they will find it difficult to engage fully not only in their work but also in their workplace relationships. That kind of situation can breed resentment and misunderstanding, fueling tensions that can further obstruct productive work relationships.

They actively work against forms of dominance and subordination that inhibit full contribution. Companies in which the third paradigm is emerging have leaders and managers who take responsibility for removing the barriers that block employees from using the full range of their competencies, cultural or otherwise. Racism, homophobia, sexism, and sexual harassment are the most obvious forms of dominance that decrease individual and organizational effectiveness—and third-paradigm leaders have zero tolerance for them. In addition, the leaders are aware that organizations can create their own unique patterns of dominance and subordination based on the presumed superiority and entitlement of some groups over others. It is not uncommon, for instance, to find organizations in which one functional area considers itself better than another. Members of the presumed inferior group frequently describe the organization in the very terms used by those who experience identity-group discrimination. Regardless of the source of the oppression, the result is diminished performance and commitment from employees.

What can leaders do to prevent those kinds of behaviors beyond explicitly forbidding any forms of dominance? They can and should test their own assumptions about the competencies of all members of the workforce because negative assumptions are often unconsciously communicated in powerful—albeit nonverbal—ways. For example, senior managers at Delta Manufacturing had for years allowed productivity and quality at their inner city plants to lag well behind the levels of other plants. When the company's chief executive officer began to question why the problem was never addressed, he came to realize that, in his heart, he had believed that inner-city workers, most of whom were African American or Hispanic, were not capable of doing better than subpar. In the end, the CEO and his senior management team were able to reverse their reasoning and take responsibility for improving the situation. The result was a sharp increase in the performance of the inner-city plants and a message to the entire organization about the capabilities of its entire workforce.

At Mastiff, the insurance company discussed earlier, the vice president and her manager decided to work with the recently promoted African American woman rather than demote her. They realized that their unit was really a pocket inside the larger organization: they did not have to wait for the rest of the organization to make a paradigm shift in order for their particular unit to change. So they met again to think about how to create conditions within their unit that would move the woman toward seeing her leadership position as encompassing all her skills. They assured her that her authentic style of leadership was precisely what they wanted her to bring to the job. They wanted her to be able to use whatever aspects of herself she thought would make her more effective in her work because the whole purpose was to do the job effectively, not to fit some preset traditional formula of how to behave. They let her know that, as a management team, they would try to adjust and change and support her. And they would deal with whatever consequences resulted from her exercising her decision rights in new ways.

Another example of this line of action—working against forms of dominance and subordination to enable full contribution—is the way the CEO of a major chemical company modified the attendance rules for his company's annual strategy conference. In the past, the conference had been attended only by senior executives, a relatively homogeneous group of white men. The company had been working hard on increasing the representation of women and people of color in its ranks, and the CEO could have left it at that. But he reckoned that, unless steps were taken, it would be ten years before the conferences tapped into the insights and perspectives of his newly diverse workforce. So he took the bold step of opening the conference to people from across all levels of the hierarchy, bringing together a diagonal slice of the organization. He also asked the conference organizers to come up with specific interventions, such as small group meetings before the larger session, to ensure that the new attendees would be comfortable enough to enter discussions. The result was that strategy-conference participants heard a much broader, richer, and livelier discussion about future scenarios for the company.

They are making sure that organizational trust stays intact. Few things are faster at killing a shift to a new way of thinking about diversity than feelings of broken trust. Therefore, managers of organizations that are successfully shifting to the learning-and-effectiveness paradigm take one more step: they make sure their organizations remain "safe" places for employees to be themselves. These managers recognize that tensions naturally arise as an organization begins to make room for diversity, starts to experiment with process and product ideas, and learns to reappraise its mission in light of suggestions from newly empowered constituents in the company. But as people put more of themselves out and open up about new feelings and ideas, the dynamics of the learning-and-effectiveness paradigm can produce temporary vulnerabilities. Managers who have helped their organizations make the change successfully have consistently demonstrated their commitment to the process and to all employees by setting a tone of honest discourse, by acknowledging tensions, and by resolving them sensitively and swiftly.

Our research over the past six years indicates that one cardinal limitation is at the root of companies' inability to attain the expected performance benefits of higher levels of diversity: the leadership's vision of the purpose of a diversified workforce. We have described the two most dominant orientations toward diversity and some of their consequences and limitations, together with a new framework for understanding and managing diversity. The learning-and-effectiveness paradigm we have outlined here is, undoubtedly, still in an emergent phase in those few organizations that embody it. We expect that as more organizations take on the challenge of truly engaging their diversity, new and unforeseen dilemmas will arise. Thus, perhaps more than anything else, a shift toward this paradigm requires a high-level commitment to learning more about the environment, structure, and tasks of one's organization, and giving improvement-generating change greater priority than the security of what is familiar. This is not an easy challenge, but we remain convinced that unless organizations take this step, any diversity initiative will fall short of fulfilling its rich promise.

The Research

THIS ARTICLE IS BASED ON a three-part research effort that began in 1990. Our subject was diversity; but, more specifically, we sought to understand three management challenges under that heading. First, how do organizations successfully achieve and sustain racial and gender diversity in their executive and middle-management ranks? Second, what is the impact of diversity on an organization's practices, processes, and performance? And, finally, how do leaders influence whether diversity becomes an enhancing or detracting element in the organization?

Over the following six years, we worked particularly closely with three organizations that had attained a high degree of demographic diversity: a small urban law firm, a community bank, and a 200-person consulting firm. In addition, we studied nine other companies in varying stages of diversifying their workforces. The group included two financial-services firms, three *Fortune* 500 manufacturing companies, two midsize high-technology companies, a private foundation, and a university medical center. In each case, we based our analysis on interviews, surveys, archival data, and observation. It is from this work that the third paradigm for managing diversity emerged and with it our belief that old and limiting assumptions about the meaning of diversity must be abandoned before its true potential can be realized as a powerful way to increase organizational effectiveness.

Originally published in September–October 1996
Reprint 96510

A Modest Manifesto for Shattering the Glass Ceiling

DEBRA E. MEYERSON AND

JOYCE K. FLETCHER

Executive Summary

ALTHOUGH WOMEN HAVE made enormous gains in
the business world—they hold seats on corporate boards
and run major companies—they still comprise only 10%
of senior managers in *Fortune 500* companies. What
will it take to shatter the glass ceiling? According to
Debra Meyerson and Joyce Fletcher, it's not a revolution
but a strategy of small wins—a series of incremental
changes aimed at the subtle discriminatory forces that still
reside in organizations.

It used to be easy to spot gender discrimination in the
corporate world, but today overt displays are rare.
Instead, discrimination against women lingers in common
work practices and cultural norms that appear unbiased.
Consider how managers have tried to rout gender discrimination in the past. Some tried to assimilate women
into the workplace by teaching them to act like men.

Others accommodated women through special policies and benefits. Still other celebrated women's differences by giving them tasks for which they are "well suited." But each of those approaches proffers solutions for the symptoms, not the sources, of gender inequity.

Gender bias, the authors say, will be undone only by a persistent campaign of incremental changes that discover and destroy the deeply embedded roots of discrimination. Because each organization is unique, its expressions of gender inequity are, too. Drawing on examples from companies that have used the small-wins approach, the authors advise readers on how they can make small wins at their own organizations. They explain why small wins will be driven by men and women together, because both will ultimately benefit from a world where gender is irrelevant to the way work is designed and distributed.

THE NEW MILLENNIUM PROVIDES an occasion to celebrate the remarkable progress made by women. That women now hold seats on corporate boards, run major companies, and are regularly featured on the covers of business magazines as prominent leaders and power brokers would have been unimaginable even a half century ago.

But the truth is, women at the highest levels of business are still rare. They comprise only 10% of senior managers in *Fortune* 500 companies; less than 4% of the uppermost ranks of CEO, president, executive vice president, and COO; and less than 3% of top corporate earners.[1] Statistics also suggest that as women approach the top of the corporate ladder, many jump off, frustrated or disillusioned with the business world. Clearly, there have been gains, but as we enter the year 2000, the glass ceiling remains. What will it take to finally shatter it?

Not a revolution. Not this time. In 1962, 1977, and even 1985, the women's movement used radical rhetoric and legal action to drive out overt discrimination, but most of the barriers that persist today are insidious—a revolution couldn't find them to blast away. Rather, gender discrimination now is so deeply embedded in organizational life as to be virtually indiscernible. Even the women who feel its impact are often hard-pressed to know what hit them.

Because the small-wins strategy creates change through diagnosis, dialogue, and experimentation, it benefits not just women but also men and the organization as a whole.

That is why we believe that the glass ceiling will be shattered in the new millennium only through a strategy that uses *small wins*[2]—incremental changes aimed at biases so entrenched in the system that they're not even noticed until they're gone. Our research shows that the small-wins strategy is a powerful way of chipping away the barriers that hold women back without sparking the kind of sound and fury that scares people into resistance. And because the small-wins strategy creates change through diagnosis, dialogue, and experimentation, it usually improves overall efficiency and performance. The strategy benefits not just women but also men and the organization as a whole.

The Problem with No Name

Time was, it was easy to spot gender discrimination in the corporate world. A respected female executive would lose a promotion to a male colleague with less experience, for instance, or a talented female manager would find herself demoted after her maternity leave. Today such blatant cases are rare; they've been wiped out by laws and by organizations' increased awareness that they have nothing to gain, and much to lose, by keeping women out of positions of authority.

That doesn't mean, however, that gender inequity has vanished. It has just gone underground. Today discrimination against women lingers in a plethora of work practices and cultural norms that only appear unbiased. They are common and mundane—and woven into the fabric of an organization's status quo—which is why most people don't notice them, let alone question them. But they create a subtle pattern of *systemic* disadvantage, which blocks all but a few women from career advancement.

For an example of this modern-day gender inequity, take the case of a global retail company based in Europe that couldn't figure out why it had so few women in senior positions and such high turnover among women in its middle-manager ranks. The problem was particularly vexing because the company's executives publicly touted their respect for women and insisted they wanted the company to be "a great place for women to work."

Despite its size, the company had a strong entrepreneurial culture. Rules and authority were informal; people were as casual about their schedules as they were about the dress code. Meetings were routinely canceled and regularly ran late. Deadlines were ignored because they constantly shifted, and new initiatives arose so frequently that people thought nothing of interrupting one another or declaring crises that demanded immediate attention.

The company's cultural norms grew from its manner of conducting business. For instance, managers were expected to be available at all times to attend delayed or emergency meetings. And these meetings themselves followed certain norms. Because roles and authority at the company were ambiguous, people felt free to make suggestions—even decisions—about any area of the company that interested them. A manager in charge of window displays, for example, might very well recommend a change in merchandising, or vice versa. To prevent changes in their own area from being made without their input, managers scrambled to attend as many meetings as possible. They had to in order to protect their turf.

The company's norms made it extraordinarily difficult for everyone—women and men—to work effectively. But they were particularly pernicious for women for two reasons. First, women typically bear a disproportionate amount of responsibility for home and family and thus have more demands on their time outside the office. Women who worked set hours—even if they spanned ten hours a day—ended up missing essential conversations and important plans for new products. Their circumscribed schedules also made them appear less committed than their male counterparts. In most instances, that was not the case, but the way the company operated day to day—its very system—made it impossible to prove otherwise.

The meetings themselves were run in a way that put women in a double bind. People often had to speak up to defend their turf, but when women did so, they were vilified. They were labeled "control freaks"; men acting the same way were called "passionate." As one female executive told us, "If you stick your neck out, you're dead."

A major investment firm provides another example of how invisible—even unintentional—gender discrimination thrives in today's companies. The firm sincerely wanted to increase the number of women it was hiring from business schools. It reasoned it would be able to hire more women if it screened more women, so it increased the number of women interviewed during recruiting visits to business school campuses. The change, however, had no impact. Why? Because, the 30 minutes allotted for each interview—the standard practice at most business schools—was not long enough for middle-aged male managers, who were conducting the vast majority of the interviews, to connect with young female candidates sufficiently to see beyond their directly relevant technical abilities. Therefore, most women were disqualified from the running. They hadn't had enough time to impress their interviewer.

The Roots of Inequity

The barriers to women's advancement in organizations today have a relatively straightforward cause. Most organizations have been created by and for men and are based on male experiences. Even though women have entered the workforce in droves in the past generation, and it is generally agreed that they add enormous value, organizational definitions of competence and leadership are still predicated on traits stereotypically associated with men: tough, aggressive, decisive. And even though many households today have working fathers and mothers, most organizations act as if the historical division of household labor still holds—with women primarily responsible for matters of the hearth. Outdated or not, those realities drive organizational life. Therefore, the global retail company was able to develop a practice of late and last-minute meetings because most men can be available 15 hours a day. The investment firm developed a practice of screening out women candidates because men, who were doing most of the interviewing, *naturally* bond with other men. In other words, organizational practices mirror societal norms.

That the "problem with no name" arises from a male-based culture does not mean that men are to blame. In fact, our perspective on gender discrimination does not presume intent, and it certainly does not assume that all men benefit from the way work is currently organized. Lots of companies run by men are working hard to create a fair environment for both sexes. And many men do not embrace the traditional division of labor; some men surely wish the conventions of a *Father Knows Best* world would vanish.

Men, then, are not to blame for the pervasive gender inequity in organizations today—but neither are women. And yet our research shows that ever since gender inequity came onto the scene as one of business's big problems, women have blamed themselves. That feeling has been reinforced by managers who have tried to solve the problem by fixing women. Indeed, over the past 30-odd years, organizations have used three approaches to rout gender discrimination, each one implying that women are somehow to blame because they "just don't fit in."

Tall People in a Short World

To describe the three approaches, we like to use a metaphor that replaces gender with height. Imagine, therefore, a world made by and for short people. In this world, everyone in power is under five-foot-five, and the most powerful are rarely taller than five-foot-three. Now imagine that after years of discrimination, tall people finally call for change—and short people agree that the current world is unfair and amends should be made.

Short people first try to right things by teaching tall people to act like short people—to minimize their differences by stooping to fit in the doorways, for example, or by hunching over to fit in the small chairs in the conference room. Once tall people learn these behaviors, short people insist, they will fit right in.

Some short people take another approach to routing discrimination: they make their world more accommodating to tall people by fixing some of the structural barriers that get in their way. They build six-foot-high doors in the back of the building and purchase desks that don't knock tall people's knees. They even go so far as to create some less demanding career paths—tall-people tracks—for those who are unwilling or unable to put up with the many realities of the short world that just can't be changed.

Other short people take a third approach: they celebrate the differences of their tall associates. Tall people stand out in a crowd, short people say, and they can reach things on high shelves. Let's recognize the worth of those skills and put them to good use! And so the short people "create equity" by putting tall people in jobs where their height is an advantage, like working in a warehouse or designing brand extensions targeted to tall people.

Those three approaches should sound familiar to anyone who has been involved in the many gender initiatives proliferating in the corporate world. Companies that take the first approach encourage women to assimilate—to adopt more masculine attributes and learn the "games their mothers never taught them." Thus, HR departments train women in assertive leadership, decision making, and even golf. Male colleagues take women to their lunch clubs, coach them on speaking up more in meetings, and suggest they take "tough guy" assignments in factories or abroad.

Companies that take the second approach accommodate the unique needs and situations of women. Many offer formal mentoring programs to compensate for women's exclusion from informal networks. Others add alternative career tracks or an extra year on the tenure clock to help women in their childbearing years. Still others offer extended maternity leave, flexible work arrangements, even rooms for nursing infants.

In the third approach, companies forgo assimilation and accommodation and instead emphasize the differences that women bring to the workplace. They institute sensitivity training to help male managers appreciate traditionally "feminine" activities or styles, such as listening and collaborating. And they eagerly put women's assumed differences to work by channeling them into jobs where they market products to women or head up HR initiatives.

All of these approaches have helped advance women's equity in the corporate world. But by now they have gone about as far as they can. Why? Because they proffer solutions that deal with the *symptoms* of gender inequity rather than the sources of inequity itself. Take the first approach. While many female executives can now play golf and have used relationships formed on the fairways to move into positions of greater power, these new skills will never eradicate the deeply entrenched, systemic factors within corporations that hold many women back.

Telling people to "value differences" doesn't mean that they will. That is why so many women who are encouraged to use "feminine" skills and styles find their efforts valued only in the most marginal sense.

The same is true of the second approach of accommodation through special policies and benefits. It gives women stilts to play on an uneven playing field, but it doesn't flatten out the field itself. So, for example, mentoring programs may help women meet key people in a company's hierarchy, but they don't change the fact that informal networks, to which few women are privy, determine who really gets resources, information, and opportunities. Launching family-friendly programs doesn't challenge the belief that balancing home and work is fundamentally a woman's problem. And adding time to a tenure clock or providing alternative career tracks does little to change the expectation that truly committed employees put work first—they need no accommodation.

The limits of the third approach are also clear. Telling people to "value differences" doesn't mean they will. That is why so many women who are encouraged to use "feminine" skills and styles find their efforts valued only in the most marginal sense. For example, women are applauded for holding teams together and are even told, "we couldn't have succeeded without you," but when promotions and rewards are distributed, they are awarded to the "rugged individuals" who assertively promoted their own ideas or came up with a onetime technical fix. Ultimately, the celebration approach may actually channel women into dead-end jobs and reinforce unhelpful stereotypes.

A Fourth Approach: Linking Equity and Effectiveness

Since 1992, we have helped organizations implement a fourth approach to eradicating gender inequity. This approach starts with the premise—to continue the metaphor—that the world of short people cannot be repaired with piecemeal fixes aimed at how tall people act and what work they do. Because the short world has been in the making for hundreds, if not thousands, of years, its assumptions and practices—such as job descriptions that conflate the physical characteristics of short people with the requirements of the job—will not be undone by assimilation or accommodation or even celebration. It will be undone by a persistent campaign of incremental changes that discover and destroy the deeply embedded roots of discrimination. These changes will be driven by short and tall people together—because both will ultimately benefit from a world where height is irrelevant to the way work is designed and distributed.

Returning to the real world of men and women, the fourth approach starts with the belief that gender inequity is rooted in our cultural patterns and therefore in our organizational systems. Although its goals are revolutionary, it doesn't advocate revolution. Instead, it emphasizes that existing systems can be reinvented by altering the raw materials of organizing—concrete, everyday practices in which biases are expressed.

The fourth approach begins when someone, somewhere in the organization realizes that the business is grappling with a gender inequity problem. Usually, the problem makes itself known through several traditional indicators. For example, recruiting efforts fail to get women to join the company in meaningful numbers; many women are stalled just before they reach leadership positions or are not rising at the same rate as their male colleagues; women

Small wins are not formulaic. Because each organization is unique, its expressions of gender inequity are, too.

tend to hold low-visibility jobs or jobs in classic "women's" departments, such as HR; senior women are waiting longer or opting to have fewer (or no) children; women have fewer resources to accomplish comparable tasks; women's pay and pay raises are not on par with men's; and women are leaving the organization at above average rates.

After recognizing that there is a problem, the next step is diagnosis. (For a description of the diagnosis stage of the small-wins strategy, see "How to Begin Small Wins" at the end of this article.) Then people must get together to talk about the work culture and determine which everyday practices are undermining effectiveness. Next, experimentation begins. Managers can launch a small initiative—or several at one time—to try to eradicate the practices that produce inequity and replace them with practices that work better for everyone. Often the experiment works—and more quickly than people would suspect. Sometimes it fixes only the symptom and loses its link to the underlying cause. When that happens, other incremental changes must be tried before a real win occurs.

Small wins are not formulaic. Each organization is unique, and its expressions of gender inequity are, too. Consider, then, how the following companies used incremental change to bring about systemic change.

Let's begin with the European retail company that was having trouble keeping its women employees. When the problem finally became impossible to ignore, the president invited us to help the organization understand what was going on. The answer wasn't immediately obvious, of course, but as we began talking to people, it became clear that it had something to do with the lack of clarity and discipline around time. Then the question was raised, Did that lack of clarity affect men and women differently? The answer was a resounding yes.

After discussing and testing the idea further, executives started using the phrase "unbounded time" to refer to meeting overruns, last-minute schedule changes, and tardiness. The term struck a chord; it quickly circulated throughout the company and sparked widespread conversation about how meeting overload and lax scheduling damaged everyone's productivity and creativity.

At that point, the president could have asked the company's female managers to become more available (assimilation). He could have mandated that all meetings take place between nine and five (accommodation). Or he could have suggested that female employees work together in projects and at times that played to their unique strengths (celebration). Instead, he and a few other senior managers quietly began to model a more disciplined use of time, and even discouraged people who suggested last-minute or late-night meetings.

Soon people began to catch on, and a new narrative started to spread through the company. The phrase "unbounded time" was used more and more often when people wanted to signal that they thought others were contributing to ineffectiveness and inequity by being late or allowing meetings to run overtime. People realized that the lack of clarity and discipline in the company had negative consequences not just for people but also for the quality of work. Over a nine-month period, norms began to shift, and as new people were hired, senior managers made sure that they understood the company was "informal *and* disciplined." To this day, the concept of "unboundedness" pops up whenever people feel the organization is slipping back into norms that silently support gender inequity.

The small-wins strategy also worked at the investment firm that tried—unsuccessfully—to hire more
women by increasing the number of interviews. After
executives realized that their 30-minute interviewing
approach was backfiring, they began to investigate their
entire recruiting practice. They examined how the questions they asked candidates, their interview procedures,
and even the places in which they were recruiting might
be giving traditional people—that is, male MBAs—an
advantage.

And so a series of small initiatives was launched. First,
the firm lengthened its interviews to 45 minutes. Partners acknowledged that shorter interviews might have
been forcing them to rely on first impressions, which are
so often a function of perceived similarity. Although
comfort level may make an interview go smoothly, it
doesn't tell you if a candidate has valuable skills, ideas,
and experience. Second, and perhaps more important,
the firm revised its interviewing protocol. In the past,
partners questioned candidates primarily about their
previous "deal experience," which allowed only those
who had worked on Wall Street to shine. Again, that
practice favored men, as most investment bank associates are men. In their new approach, managers followed
a set protocol and began asking candidates to talk about
how they would contribute to the firm's mission. The
interviews shifted radically in tone and substance.
Instead of boasting from former Wall Street stars, they
heard many nontraditional candidates—both women
and men—describe a panoply of managerial skills, creative experiences, and diverse work styles. And indeed,
these people are bringing new energy and talent into the
firm. (As an added bonus, the following year the firm
arrived at one prominent business school to find it was

earning a reputation as a great place to work, making its recruiting efforts even more fruitful.)

Both the retail company and investment firm saw their equity and performance improve after implementing changes in their systems that could hardly be called radical. The same kind of success story can be told about an international scientific research institute. The institute, which produces new agricultural technologies for farmers, had a strong cultural norm of rewarding individual achievement. When a breakthrough was reached, a new product was developed, or a grant was won, individual scientists usually got the credit and rewards. The norm meant that support work by secretaries and technicians, as well as by scientists and professionals in departments like biotechnology and economics, was often ignored.

Paradoxically, top-level managers at the institute spoke enthusiastically about the value of teamwork and asserted that success was a group, not an individual, product. In fact, the organization planned to move to a team-based structure because senior managers considered it an imperative for addressing complex cross-functional challenges. But in the everyday workings of the organization, no one paid much heed to supporting contributors. The stars were individual "heroes."

The undervaluation of support work was an issue that affected many women because they were more likely to be in staff positions or scientific roles that were perceived as support disciplines. In addition, women more often took on support work because they were expected to do so or because they felt it was critical to a project's success. They connected people with one another, for instance, smoothed disagreements, facilitated teamwork, and taught employees new skills.

Many women expressed frustration with this type of work because it simply wasn't recognized or rewarded. Yet they were reluctant to stop because the costs of not doing it were clear to them. Without it, information would flow less easily, people would miss deadlines, more crises would erupt, and teams would break down. As we talked with them, women began to recognize the value of their efforts, and they gave them a name: "invisible work."

As in the European retail company, naming the problem had a striking effect. It turned out that invisible work wasn't just a problem for women. Men and women started talking about how the lack of value placed on invisible work was related to much larger systemic patterns. For example, people noted that the company tended to give sole credit for projects to the lead scientists, even when others had contributed or had helped spare the projects from major crises. People, especially women, admitted that mentors and bosses had advised them—and they had often advised one another—to avoid taking on invisible work to focus on work that would afford more recognition. Stemming from these informal discussions, a narrative about the importance of invisible work began to spread throughout the organization.

For senior managers who saw the link between invisible work and their goal of moving to a team-based structure, the challenge was to find ways to make invisible work visible—and to ensure it was valued and more widely shared by men and women. A task force on the topic proposed a new organizationwide evaluation system that would gather input from peers and direct reports—people to whom an employee's invisible work is visible. Although that step seemed insignificant to many, it was approved and launched.

Several years later, people say that the institute is a different place. The first small win—the new evaluation process—gave way to others, such as a new process to increase information flow up, down, and sideways; new criteria for team leaders that emphasize facilitation rather than direction; and new norms about tapping expertise, no matter where it resides in the hierarchy. Implicitly, these changes challenged the prevailing masculine, individualist image of competence and leadership and opened the way for alternatives more conducive to teamwork. Today both men and women say there is a stronger sense of fairness. And senior managers say that the systemic changes brought about by the small-wins strategy were central to the institute's successful move to a team-based structure.

Small Wins Can Make Big Gains

It's surprising how quickly people can come up with ideas for small wins—and how quickly they can be put into action. Take, for example, the case of the finance department at a large manufacturing company. The department had a strong norm of *overdoing* work. Whenever senior managers asked for information, the department's analysts would generate multiple scenarios complete with sophisticated graphs and charts.

The fact was, however, senior managers often only wanted an analyst's back-of-the-envelope estimates. People in the finance department even suspected as much, but there was an unspoken policy of never asking the question. The reasons? First, they worried that questions would indicate that they couldn't figure out the scope of the request themselves and hence were not competent. Second, many of the requests came in at the end of the day. Analysts feared that asking, "How much detail do you want?" might look like a way to avoid working late. To show their commitment, they felt they had to stay and give every request the full treatment.

The norm of devoting hours on end to each request hit women in the department especially hard. As women in an industry dominated by men, they felt they had to work extra hard to demonstrate their competence and commitment, especially when commitment was measured, at least in part, by time spent at work. However, the norm negatively affected men, too. The extra work, simply put, was a waste of time; it lowered productivity and dampened enthusiasm. The organization suffered: talented people avoided the department because of its reputation for overtime.

The small-wins process at this company began when we met with a group of analysts and managers in the finance department. We presented our diagnosis of the root causes of the overwork problem and asked if they could come up with small, concrete solutions to counteract it. It didn't take them long. Within an hour, the analysts had designed a one-page form that asked senior managers to describe the parameters of each request. How much detail was required? What was the desired output? The form very simply took the onus off individuals to ask taboo questions, relieving women of the fear that they might appear less than committed and allowing all analysts—not just women—to use their time more productively.

Interestingly, after only a short time, the form was dropped. Analysts reported that simply having a conversation with their managers about the company's norms and taboos changed the department's dynamics. By establishing an open dialogue, analysts could now ask clarifying questions without fearing that they were signaling incompetence or lack of commitment.

Small wins make sense even at companies that already have programs designed to combat gender inequity. Consider the case of a New York advertising agency that was particularly proud of its mentoring program aimed at developing high-potential female leaders. Although that program got women's names into the mix, the jobs that women were ultimately offered tended to be in human resource-type positions—positions women were thought to be particularly well suited for. These jobs often required a high level of skill, but their lack of rainmaking potential resulted in career disadvantages that accumulated over time.

The situation was compounded by an unspoken rule at the company of never saying no to developmental opportunities. This norm, like so many others, seems gender neutral. It appears to be a risk for both men and women to pass up opportunities, particularly those offered in the name of developing leadership potential. Yet because of the different types of opportunities offered, women stood to lose whether they said yes or no. Saying no signaled lack of commitment. But saying yes meant they would spend valuable time and energy doing a job that was unlikely to yield the same career benefits that men were deriving from the opportunities offered to them. What made the situation particularly problematic for the organization was that the HR-type

The reason small wins work so effectively is that they are not random efforts. They unearth and upend systemic barriers to women's progress.

jobs that women were reluctant to accept were often critical to overall functioning.

The women in the mentoring programs were the first to realize the negative impact of the company's informal policy of channeling women into these critical HR positions. So they got together to brainstorm about ways to extricate themselves from their double bind. (Like many small-wins campaigns, this one was launched with the knowledge and approval of senior management. For ideas on how to start the change process without official sanction, see "Going It Alone" at the end of this article.) The women coached one another on how to respond to the HR-type job offers in ways that would do minimal damage to their careers. For instance, they came up with the solution of accepting the job with the stipulation that senior managers assign its year-end objectives a "rainmaking equivalency quotient." The group pushed senior managers to think about the underlying assumptions of putting women in HR jobs. Did they really believe men could not manage people? If so, didn't that mean that men should be given the developmental opportunities in HR? These questions led senior managers to several revelations, which were especially important since the organization had recently decided to sell itself to potential clients as the relationship-oriented alternative to other agencies. The full effect of this small-win effort, launched recently, will likely be seen over the course of the next few years.

The Power of Small Wins

Small wins are not silver bullets; anyone familiar with real organizational change knows that there is no such thing. Rather, the reason small wins work so effectively is that they are not random efforts. They unearth and upend systemic barriers to women's progress. Consider how:

First, small wins tied to the fourth approach help organizations give a name to practices and assumptions that are so subtle they are rarely questioned, let alone seen as the root of organizational ineffectiveness. When the retail company started using the phrase "unbounded time," people began developing a shared understanding of how the lack of discipline around time affected men and women differently and how the lack of boundaries in the culture contributed to people's inability to get work accomplished. The act of naming the "problem with no name" opens up the possibility of change.

Second, small wins combine changes in behavior with changes in understanding. When a small win works— when it makes even a minor difference in systemic prac- tices—it helps to verify a larger theory. It says that some- thing bigger is going on.

Third, and related, small wins tie the local to the global. That is, people involved in small wins see how their efforts affect larger, systemic change, in much the same way as people taking part in small-town recycling campaigns come to understand their impact in decreas- ing global warming. This big-picture outlook is both energizing and self-reinforcing, and it links seemingly unrelated small wins together.

Fourth, small wins have a way of snowballing. One small change begets another, and eventually these small changes add up to a whole new system. Consider again the investment firm that revised its recruiting processes. It realized that something as simple as lengthening interview time could begin to address its recruitment problem. But if it had stopped there, it is unlikely that fundamental changes would have occurred. Recognizing why the length of an interview was an issue—how "feeling comfortable" and "fitting the mold" had been implicit selection criteria—helped the firm make additional, more substantial changes in, for instance, the questions asked. This change is encouraging the executives to look into initiatives to revise other practices, ranging from publicity to training, that also held hidden biases, not just for women but also for other underrepresented groups.

The fifth and final source of power in the small-wins approach is that it routs discrimination by fixing the organization, not the women who work for it. In that way, it frees women from feelings of self-blame and anger that can come with invisible inequity. And it removes the label of troublemaker from women who complain that something is not right. Small wins say, "Yes, something is wrong. It is the organization itself, and when it is fixed, all will benefit."

As we enter the new millennium, we believe that it is time for new metaphors to capture the subtle, systemic forms of discrimination that still linger. It's not the ceiling that's holding women back; it's the whole structure of the organizations in which we work: the foundation, the beams, the walls, the very air. The barriers to advancement are not just above women, they are all around them. But dismantling our organizations isn't the solution. We must ferret out the hidden barriers to equity and effectiveness one by one. The fourth approach asks leaders to act as thoughtful architects and to reconstruct buildings beam by beam, room by room, rebuilding with practices that are stronger and more equitable, not just for women but for all people.

The Research: A Joint Effort

THE RESEARCH FOR THIS ARTICLE began in 1992 and is ongoing. Our work—including interviews, surveys, archival data, focus groups, and observations—has taken place at 11 organizations. They included three *Fortune* 500 companies, two international research organizations, two public agencies, a global retail organization, an investment firm, a school, and a private foundation. The goal of each project was to create the kind of small wins and learning reported in this article.

The ideas presented in this article were developed in collaboration with three colleagues: Robin Ely, an associate professor at Columbia University's School of International and Public Affairs in New York City and an affiliated faculty member at the Center for Gender in Organizations, Simmons Graduate School of Management, in Boston; Deborah Kolb, a codirector of the Center for Gender in Organizations, a professor of management at Simmons Graduate School of Management, and a senior fellow at the Program on Negotiation at Harvard Law School; and anthropologist Deborah Merrill-Sands, a codirector of the Center for Gender in Organizations and an expert in conducting research on gender in organizations.

The research in this article builds directly on the foundational work of Lotte Bailyn, the T. Wilson Professor of Management at the MIT Sloan School of Management in Cambridge, Massachusetts, and Rhona Rapoport, director of the Institute of Family and Environmental Research in London. They also collaborated on many of the projects mentioned in this article.

How to Begin Small Wins

ONCE AN ORGANIZATION determines that it has a problem—female employees won't join the company, say, or women are leaving in alarming numbers—it is time to start searching for causes. Such diagnosis involves senior managers probing an organization's practices and beliefs to uncover its deeply embedded sources of inequity. But how?

An effective first step is often one-on-one interviews with employees to uncover practices and beliefs in the company's culture—how work gets done, for instance, what activities are valued, and what the assumptions are about competence. After that, focus groups can more closely examine questionable practices. Some companies have found it useful to have women and men meet separately for these initial discussions, as long as the outcomes of these meetings are shared.

Diagnosis isn't always straightforward. After all, the group is looking for the source of a relatively invisible problem. Yet we have found a collection of questions that help keep the process on track:

- How do people in this organization accomplish their work? What, if anything, gets in the way?
- Who succeeds in this organization? Who doesn't?
- How and when do we interact with one another? Who participates? Who doesn't?
- What kinds of work and work styles are valued in this organization? What kinds are invisible?
- What is expected of leaders in this company?
- What are the norms about time in this organization?

- What aspects of individual performance are discussed the most in evaluations?

- How is competence identified during hiring and performance evaluations?

After the initial diagnosis, managers should identify cultural patterns and their consequences. For example, Which practices affect men differently than women, and why? Which ones have unintended consequences for the business? Following this analysis, change agents can discuss these patterns with different people. We call this stage "holding up the mirror," and it represents the first part of developing a new shared narrative in the organization.

The next step, of course, is designing the small wins. We have found that by this point in the process, groups usually have little trouble identifying ways to make concrete changes. It is critical, however, that the managers guiding the process keep the number and scope of initiatives relatively limited and strategically targeted. Managers and other change agents should remind the organization that a single experiment should not be seen as an end in itself. Each small win is a trial intervention and a probe for learning, intended not to overturn the system but to slowly and surely make it better.

Going It Alone

ONE OF THE MOST IMPORTANT virtues of the fourth approach is that it helps people realize that they are not alone: the problems are systemic, not individual. That said, individuals or small groups may still have to "go it alone" without the support of an organizational mandate or formal change program. Although first efforts are aimed at subverting the status quo, over time they may, in fact, be embraced by the organization because they create the impetus for learning and positive change.

Individuals can adopt one of two methods. First, they can simply operate solo. They can conduct a diagnosis, identify sources of gender discrimination, and design small wins themselves. That approach is hard, as the process depends so heavily on frank discussion and testing of ideas. That is why we suggest that individuals use a second method: finding like minds to join them in the exercise. The group can be internal to the organization or it can include people from various organizations. It can include only women or it can include women and men. The point is to hear one another's stories about workplace practices and their consequences in order to discover common themes and underlying factors. Small groups can generate small wins on their own and experiment with them quietly but persistently.

So often, the "problem with no name" is experienced by women as a situation that affects them alone or worse, as a problem with them. In our executive education programs, we have seen that when women share their experiences, they recognize that many of the problems they experience as individuals are actually systemic and not unique to them or to their organization. And they realize that promoting change can benefit the organization as well as the men and women in it. That insight motivates them to work on their own and in collaboration with others to create small wins that can make a big difference.

Notes

1. Statistics on women of color are even more drastic. Although women of color make up 23% of the U.S. women's workforce, they account for only 14% of women in managerial roles. African-American women comprise only 6% of the women in managerial roles.

2. The small-wins approach to change was developed by Karl Weick. See "Small Wins: Redefining the Scale of Social Problems," *American Psychologist*, 1984.

Originally published in January–February 2000
Reprint R00107

Mommy-Track Backlash

ALDEN M. HAYASHI

Executive Summary

"PLEASE DON'T TELL ME that I need to have a baby to have this time off." Those words were still ringing in the ears of Jessica Gonon an hour after a tense meeting with Jana Rowe, one of her key account managers.

Jessica, the vice president of sales and customer support at ClarityBase, considered Jana's request for a four-day workweek, for which she was willing to take a corresponding 20% cut in pay. Although the facts seemed simple, the situation was anything but. Just last week, Davis Bennett, another account manager, had made a similar request. He wanted a lighter workload so he could train for the Ironman Triathlon World Championship. Both Jana and Davis were well aware that Megan Flood, another account manager, had been working a reduced schedule for nearly two years. When she was hired, Megan had requested Fridays off to spend time with her two young sons. And since she came highly recommended and the talent pool was tight, Jessica agreed to the arrangement.

The eight account managers at ClarityBase were in charge of helping the company's largest clients install and maintain database applications, which often required no small amount of hand-holding and coddling. Because Megan had an abbreviated schedule, the other account managers were assigned the more difficult clients. But if Jessica agreed to a shorter workweek for Jana and Davis, who would take on the toughest customers? And what would happen if the other account managers started asking for similar deals?

How can Jessica maintain the productivity of her department and meet her staff's needs for flexible work schedules while striking an equitable solution for both parents and nonparents? Four experts advise Jessica on her next move in this fictional case study.

"PLEASE DON'T TELL ME that I need to have a baby to have this time off." Those words were still ringing in the ears of Jessica Gonon an hour after a tense meeting with one of her key managers. As she sat in her office trying to make sense of a recent customer survey, Jessica, the vice president of sales and customer support at ClarityBase, was having trouble concentrating on the bar graphs and pie charts in front of her. Snippets from her earlier conversation kept interrupting her thoughts.

The issue seemed simple enough. Jana Rowe, an account manager in the sales support department, had requested a lighter workload: she wanted a four-day workweek, and for that she was willing to take a corresponding 20% cut in pay. Those were the simple facts, but the situation at ClarityBase was anything but straightforward.

Just last week, Davis Bennett, another account manager, had made a similar request. He wanted a lighter workload so he could train for the Ironman Triathlon World Championship, the premier competition held each October in Hawaii. He was a world-class athlete, and his ultimate goal was a spot on the U.S. Olympic team in 2004. Davis had said he didn't need to begin training full throttle until mid-spring, so Jessica had asked him for a couple weeks to figure out how Clarity-Base might best accommodate his training schedule.

A complicating factor was that both Davis and Jana were well aware that Megan Flood, another account manager, had been working a reduced schedule for nearly two years. When she was hired, Megan had requested Fridays off to spend time with her two young boys, and Jessica had agreed.

In her meeting with Jessica, Jana had declined to explain why she wanted the reduced hours, citing "personal reasons." When Jessica had paused, wondering what those reasons might be, Jana added, "All I'm asking for is the same deal that Megan has. Please don't tell me that I need to have a baby to have this time off." Jana was married and had no children. Davis was single and also without children.

There were other subtle issues. A reduced workweek for Jana and Davis meant much more than just that. From Jessica's conversations with them, she inferred that any official reduction in hours—having a day off every week in Jana's case—would also mean they wouldn't have to work the occasional nights and weekends that the other account managers did, all except Megan.

ClarityBase, headquartered in Reston, Virginia, sold large database applications that helped companies run their operations, including human resources, manufacturing, and order fulfillment. The eight account managers—Jana, Davis, and Megan among them—were in charge of helping the company's largest customers install and maintain the software, which required no small amount of handholding and coddling. Because Megan had an abbreviated workweek, the other account managers were assigned the more demanding clients.

If Jessica agreed to a shorter workweek for Jana and Davis, who would take over clients like St. Elizabeth's? And what would happen if the other account managers began asking for similar deals?

Davis, in particular, seemed to have the toughest customers, most notably St. Elizabeth's Hospital in Philadelphia, which required him to be available around-the-clock. Once, when its system failed on Christmas Day, Davis took the train to Philadelphia to help get the hospital's crucial patient database up and running. If Jessica agreed to a shorter workweek for Jana and Davis, who would take over clients like St. Elizabeth's? And what would happen if the other account managers began asking for similar deals?

It was Monday morning—what a way to start the week, thought Jessica. She had promised Jana that she'd get back to her by Friday, so at least she had the whole week to sort things out. That was plenty of time, or so she hoped.

Trading Places

Jessica had had second thoughts before hiring Megan—she had made so many demands in the interview. Her children, said Megan, were paramount to her, and she wanted a very flexible schedule. Not only did she want the freedom to come in late and leave early occasionally, she also wanted Fridays off. She wasn't amenable to any business travel, and she wouldn't be able to attend after-hours meetings except when her personal schedule allowed.

But Megan had come highly recommended. Her three years of experience at Dawson Software, Clarity-Base's chief competitor, would be a huge asset; her technical skills were superb; and her professional and friendly demeanor would surely impress customers. And, last but certainly not least, Jessica had looked for months to hire someone of Megan's caliber. None of the other candidates had come remotely close. So after thinking about it over a weekend, Jessica decided to offer her the job.

Still, Megan's demands had left Jessica feeling uneasy. Part of the reason, Jessica realized later after much introspection, was because she had had it much tougher when she was starting her career in the early 1970s—a different era before flexible work hours, on-site day care centers, and the Family and Medical Leave Act. At that time, women like Jessica, who held a bachelor's degree in computer programming from Penn State, simply couldn't have it all, both career and children. So Jessica and her husband, who was on the partner track at his architectural firm, had decided that she would quit her job as a supervisor in the MIS department for Capital Insurance when they had their first child.

Nine years later, after their youngest child had started kindergarten, Jessica reentered the workforce as a sales assistant at ClarityBase. She took classes at night to get up to speed on the computer industry and slowly rose to become a sales rep, then account manager, and then head of the Northeast sales region. At the age of 52, she was promoted to her current position of vice president of sales and customer support. The road had been long, and having children had been a substantial detour. But just because Jessica had had to make trade-offs between career and family, should Megan have to as well?

ClarityBase prided itself on its progressive work-life policies. But had the company become too pro-parent at the expense of other employees?

Hidden Tensions

It was nearly 7 PM when Jessica finally crammed the customer survey reports into her briefcase and started to head home. As she walked through the sales-support group, she was reminded of a conversation she happened to overhear in this corridor last week: "I honestly don't know if I can force myself to smile through yet another precious baby shower," said a woman's voice from the other side of a cubicle wall. At the time, Jessica paid little attention to the comment, but now, those words made her stop and think.

ClarityBase prided itself on its progressive work-life policies. The company offered all employees family medical insurance, adoption assistance, and paid maternity and paternity leave. But perhaps the thing that ClarityBase was most proud of was the on-site child care center that the company subsidized. Bill Welensky, vice president of human resources, liked to brag that such perks helped ClarityBase keep employee turnover to less than 5% annually, unheard of in the software industry. But

had the company become too pro-parent at the expense
of other employees?

A year and a half ago, as Labor Day approached, tension between the two groups surfaced. Ed Fernandez—
whom Jessica had just hired to supervise ClarityBase's
call center—had drawn up the schedule for the holiday
weekend in what he thought was the fairest way: people
who hadn't worked over a holiday for the longest time
would be the first to be called to duty. Many mothers
were on the short list because the previous supervisor
had never scheduled them to work on holidays. When
the assignments were posted, the mothers were peeved,
and their reaction irritated other employees.

Fortunately, Ed was able to strike a compromise. The
assignments for Labor Day would be done as they had
been in the past, with special consideration given to
mothers. From that point on, though, every employee
would have to work his or her fair share of holidays,
regardless of past status or history. The only consideration would be for seniority: newer employees, whether
they were parents or not, would be the first to serve.

That solution seemed to prevent a fracture in the
workplace between parents and nonparents. But could
it be that a dangerous rift did exist, with only a fragile
veneer of social decorum to conceal it? Jessica did an
about-face and headed back to her office to reboot her
computer. She composed two e-mails, one to Jana and the
other to Davis, requesting that she meet with each of
them as soon as possible to discuss their requests further.

Gathering Information

At lunch the next day, Jessica waited until she and Jana
had comfortably settled into their booth and ordered

their meals before asking the delicate question. "I want to understand your situation, why you've requested a shorter workweek," she started. "Yesterday, you cited 'personal reasons.' The last thing I want to do is pry into your personal life, but is there anything else you would feel comfortable telling me?"

Jessica watched as Jana swallowed her food and collected her thoughts. "I don't mean to be disrespectful," Jana began. "Honestly, I don't. Nor do I mean to be mysterious. But I really don't think I should have to explain why I want the time off. Suffice it to say that it's very, very important to me."

"I see," replied Jessica. "I'm sorry to have asked. I just wanted to understand your situation better."

The two women ate in silence for a few minutes. Then Jana put her fork down and looked at Jessica intently. "The thing that gets me," Jana said, "is that somehow all the family stuff is deemed more important—the soccer games, the school plays, the graduations. Well, I have important things going on in my life, too. They just don't involve children."

"Do you think that parents are treated with favoritism at ClarityBase?" Jessica asked.

"I'd like to think not," Jana replied. "But is it so hard to believe that my reasons for wanting a lighter workload might be just as important to me as Megan's children are to her?" Before Jessica could say anything, Jana added, "Don't get me wrong. I think Megan's great. She's one of our best account managers, so I have no qualms about the deal she has. I'm just saying that I think I deserve the same deal."

On her drive home that night, Jessica thought more about what Jana had said. She had heard of companies with a no-explanation policy for time off, but that blanket policy seemed unfair to her. Some people might need more consideration at a specific time—for example, the birth of a child—whereas others could postpone their plans—for instance, a college course could be taken in the fall instead of in the spring. On the other hand, a blanket no-explanation policy would certainly make her job easier—she wouldn't have to make value judgments about whose reasons were more important.

Breakfast the next morning with Davis went more smoothly. When Jessica asked him whether he felt that parents at ClarityBase were treated with favoritism, he replied, "I've never felt like a second-class citizen, if that's what you're asking. I really don't mind helping out someone who's having some kind of family emergency, because working parents have it tough. I have no idea how they juggle everything. I'd be a nut case."

"Thanks for your great attitude," said Jessica.

"Well, we're all on the same team."

"I guess what I need to know from you," Jessica continued, "is how much flexibility you might have. Excuse my ignorance, but I know very little about triathletes, and I'm not sure how much time off you'll need to train."

"It varies; everyone seems to have a different training regimen," said Davis. "But here's what I think would work best for me: for the summer, I'd like to leave work at 3 on Tuesdays and Thursdays. Then, during the fall, I'd want to leave early maybe four days a week. But on the days I left early, I could definitely come in at 6 AM to make up some of that time, or I could stay later on the other days."

"I appreciate that," said Jessica, "and I've always been grateful for your willingness to go the extra mile. But with this new schedule, do you think you could keep up with the needs of your clients?"

"I've thought about that a lot and, to be honest with you, I don't know," Davis admitted. "I realize that the customer comes first, but I'd also like to think that most of them would be willing to make adjustments—and I think they'd be minor ones—to accommodate my new hours. Of course, I have no idea if everything would work out as smoothly as I'm hoping."

"This particular triathlon is really important to you?" Jessica asked, almost rhetorically.

"Well, I've won a few local ones, but nothing big," said Davis. "And the Ironman is big; it's the Superbowl. My goal is to place in the top 20. And, yes, it's very important to me. In fact, I suppose I've never wanted anything as badly in my entire life."

Jessica thought back to when she had hired Davis more than five years ago. What impressed her most about him was his passion. Davis was clearly the type of person who threw himself into everything he did, and it was evident in his work. So it was hardly surprising that he would want extra training time to prepare for the Ironman.

Decision Time

As Jessica pulled into ClarityBase's parking lot, she noticed a Honda with a bumper sticker that proudly declared "Child-*free* (not child-*less*)...and loving every minute of it." Could that car belong to the woman she had overheard the other night?

Before heading to her office, Jessica decided to stop by the HR department to talk with Bill Welensky. "Bill, do you have a few free minutes?" she asked.

Bill, who was Jessica's mentor and one of her biggest supporters at ClarityBase, listened carefully as she told him about Jana, Davis, and her earlier arrangement with Megan. "I know that we don't have any official policy that specifically addresses these issues," she said, "but I was hoping for some advice."

"I'm not sure exactly what to say," said Bill. "As you know, ClarityBase prides itself on its progressive views on work-life issues, and we try to accommodate people as much as possible. But we really don't have any policies at all regarding flex time."

When Jessica told Bill about what Jana had said—that she felt parents got special consideration at ClarityBase—he paused before speaking. "That's not the first time that sentiment has been expressed," he offered. "But as far as flex time or shorter workweeks are concerned, we certainly don't have any guidelines with regard to parents versus nonparents. Supervisors just have to make those kinds of decisions on a case by case basis."

"I feel like I somehow have to make value judgments about what's more important, someone's parenting needs versus someone else's personal achievement goals."

Jessica thought about that for a few seconds. "The problem," she started, "is that I feel like I somehow have to make value judgments about what's more important, someone's parenting needs versus someone else's personal achievement goals. And I don't feel comfortable doing that."

Bill looked at Jessica. "Have you tried taking a different perspective?" he asked. "Think of it as two employees who both want raises but your budget will allow just one. What would you do?"

Without hesitation, Jessica replied, "I'd make a judgment about just how valuable—and irreplaceable—each

employee was. But my situation is so much more complicated than that. With salary requests, I could compare
apples with apples. With work-life issues, I feel like I have
to compare an apple with a hammer with a vase."

"Then let me speak to you as a friend and not as the
HR director," Bill said. "And let me be frank with you: the
reason you were promoted to vice president is precisely
because of your ability to compare apples with hammers
and vases. You run a large department and, yes, it's not
always easy to meet the needs of your staff while also
making your quarterly numbers. So, no, you can't go out
and hire two more account managers to cover for the
people who want flex time. There is no simple, tidy solution here."

As Jessica left Bill's office, she tried to reassure herself
that it was just Wednesday; she still had until Friday to
figure out what to do. The problem, though, was that
with each day she was becoming increasingly confused.

How should Jessica stem the backlash?

Four commentators offer their advice.

MICHELE S. DARLING *is the executive vice president
of corporate governance and human resources at Prudential Insurance Company of America in Newark,
New Jersey.*

Jessica Gonon needs an entirely new mind-set. She
has been shouldering too much on her own. But she
doesn't need to figure out how to make flexible schedules
work, her staff does. If they want flexible schedules, they
need to devise ways to make them work within the context of achieving the department's business goals and
objectives.

When Davis Bennett, for example, made his request, Jessica asked him very reasonable questions, such as whether he could continue to meet the needs of his clients. But his response was that he wasn't sure, as if it were now her problem to solve. It's not. If Davis and Jana Rowe want to change their schedules, they need to figure out how to make that work.

From my experience, I believe that no corporate policies, programs, or guidelines can cover all of the myriad work-life situations that are bound to arise. And I have found that, nine times out of ten, people will come up with more creative and better solutions for meeting their needs for flexible work hours than their managers or someone sitting in my chair could have.

That said, Jessica should provide the tools her people will need to make their strongest cases for flexible time. She should start by sitting down with Bill Welensky of HR to devise guidelines for employee proposals for flexible work arrangements. The format should specify what each proposal must contain: what work needs to be managed during this period of time, how the person will do that work so that the schedule is seamless to customers, what hours the person is proposing to work, and so on.

She should give Jana and Davis the guidelines and encourage them to think of creative ways of achieving flexibility while also getting their jobs done. She should suggest that they consider as many options as possible, such as telecommuting and job sharing with another account manager.

Since Jessica has realized that a rift between parents and nonparents might be developing in her department, she should call a departmental meeting to tell people that she is open to flexible work hours for everyone, regardless of their reasons for wanting them. But, she should add, it's up to each individual to make a strong business case for the change. "As far as I'm concerned," Jessica might say, "the reason for your request is irrelevant. I don't care if you want to leave early on Wednesdays to take your son to baseball practice or to take a class. You just need to explain how you're going to continue to get your work done."

When Jessica declines a request, she needs to give specific reasons for her decision. Perhaps the applicant hasn't sufficiently demonstrated how he will meet his customers' needs. Or maybe the employee fails to explain the details of her job-sharing arrangement. Jessica should then give the person a chance to revise the proposal for her reconsideration.

Jessica might also encourage her eight account managers to think as a team. Collectively, they might devise a new way to get their work done while also ensuring that their personal needs are being met. Again, Jessica might offer suggestions, such as having two or more account managers for demanding customers like St. Elizabeth's Hospital.

Of course, for many situations, flexible arrangements are inherently difficult, such as with call-center operations. Even then, however, people often come up with effective solutions. At Prudential Insurance, we have found that telecommuting can work even for employees in a call center. With the right technology, it doesn't matter where the employee is physically located.

Jessica's task won't be easy. But by encouraging her staff to come up with creative solutions, she can go a long way toward meeting their needs.

CHRIS DINEEN *is the director of finance at RadView Software in Burlington, Massachusetts.*

Jessica's confusion is understandable. Like many companies, ClarityBase has tried to create a family-friendly environment, but it hasn't developed any overall guidelines or policies to do so. Jessica needs to examine her situation from the inside out, starting with the trees before tending to the forest.

At its core, the problem is simple—Jessica must maintain the performance of her department while ensuring that the members of her staff are content with the balance they have struck between their professional and personal lives. Obviously, Jessica must first determine just how many of her account managers can be on a reduced workload.

Let's assume that Jessica's department can afford to have only one additional person on a reduced workload, so she needs to decide between Jana and Davis. Jessica attempted to learn why each of them desired a reduced schedule to help her base her decision on whose situation had greater merit. While Davis was forthcoming in explaining the reason for his request, Jana chose to keep her details confidential. Understandably, Jessica doesn't want to pry into Jana's personal life, but this information could be crucial. Consider an extreme example: what if Jana wanted Wednesdays free so that she could do some freelance work for a competitor of ClarityBase?

Bill, the head of HR, suggested that Jessica view her dilemma from a different perspective by thinking of two employees who both want a raise that only one of them can have. If Jana asked Jessica for a salary increase without being able to justify her request, Jessica would have little difficulty saying no. In other words, both Jana and Davis need to make their strongest cases for their requests for reduced hours, and Jessica must then decide between them. If Jana, for whatever reason, fails to present a compelling case, then Jessica has no other choice but to make a decision based on the limited information she has.

But there might be a larger issue here. Megan, the working mother, is generally precluded from working evenings and weekends because of family obligations. Perhaps Jana's request is really a protest against having to bear the burden of longer hours and tougher clients. Jana may see a reduced workload as the only way to resolve what she perceives as unfair work allocation.

That said, Jessica should explore alternatives to achieve an equitable solution among *all* of the account managers, both parents and nonparents. Not that she should renege on her deal with Megan—after all, Megan joined ClarityBase with the understanding that the company would accommodate her parenting needs. But maybe Jessica could implement a policy in which account managers accumulate overtime hours that they can use later for time off. Or she might consider giving additional compensation, such as bonuses and raises, to employees bearing a heavier burden of the workload—if she isn't already doing so.

Jessica also has to consider the broad impact of her decisions. If Megan, Jessica, and Davis worked reduced hours, would others on her staff insist on the same thing? More generally, would employees in other departments also seek to receive similarly reduced workloads?

Thinking about those questions, Jessica can now begin to look at the forest. She'll need to let Bill know what she's doing because her actions may very well set a de facto policy for the rest of ClarityBase. Perhaps it is now Jessica's turn to give Bill some advice: he should quickly call a meeting of the senior executives at Clarity-Base to discuss the company's need to establish official policies and guidelines on work-life and family issues. Otherwise, managers like Jessica will be creating those policies in an ad hoc fashion.

ELINOR BURKETT *is the author of* The Baby Boon: How Family-Friendly America Cheats the Childless *(Free Press, 2000). She is a journalist, and her articles have appeared in the* Miami Herald, New York Times Magazine, *the* Atlantic Monthly, Rolling Stone, *and* Mirabella.

Jessica is confronted with one of the stickiest issues in HR today: how to clean up the mess created by an ill-considered rush into family-friendly workplaces. When businesses like ClarityBase began offering special considerations to working parents, they failed to consider that granting one group of employees such privileges adds up, perforce, to inferior treatment for the rest of the workforce.

Of course, employers have long engaged in inequitable practices, but they have traditionally done so to encourage and reward merit or tenure—*not* worker fertility. If you consider the dollar value of ClarityBase's benefits packages as a form of compensation, you'll quickly see that the company has changed those rules. As a result, employees like Jana and Davis know that no matter how hard, long, or well they work, they can't achieve remunerative parity with their peers who are parents. Even if they were to receive huge merit bonuses and salary raises, their total compensation would still fall short of what they would have been receiving had they been parents doing the same work.

That's no way to maintain employee morale. Ask any manager of a Marxist enterprise who tried to run a business guided by the principle "from each according to his ability, to each according to his need." The result has typically been employee apathy, which leads to lackluster performance. After all, why go the extra mile when it won't be rewarded?

In trying to resolve the dilemma created by her company's departure from a merit-based compensation system, Jessica was right to cringe from standing in judgment on the relative value of what her employees proposed to do with their requested time off. Doing so is not only a dangerous invasion of employee privacy; it is demeaning, particularly in a diverse society. Should a gay employee with a sick partner be forced to come out to get leave to care for him? Should a Mormon staffer have to explain the importance of working one day a week as a missionary?

Executives who manage their workforces in that fashion set themselves up as the applause meter in the old TV game show *Queen for a Day*, with staff members forced to compete for the title of "employee most needy of consideration." But workplace benefits should not be contest prizes; they should be rewards for jobs well done.

And that is precisely the solution to Jessica's conundrum: she needs to recognize that benefits and flexibility are as integral to employee compensation packages as are paychecks, and she must uniformly apply the time-proven standard of equal pay for equal work when handing out assignments and perks. "Pay is for work done, rather than for the number of dependents of the workers," asserted Secretary of Labor Lewis Baxter Schwellenbach in the 1940s, when he argued for the Equal Pay Act. A company that adheres to that standard does not adjust the salaries of people according to their number of dependents, nor does it limit health insurance benefits only to workers with kids. Similarly, businesses must treat time and other nonfinancial benefits with the same dependent-neutral hand.

So Jessica needn't think about the relative merits of what her employees do with their free time; that is not her legitimate concern. Instead, she should judge the relative value of those employees in the workplace context, which is most certainly her business, and reward them accordingly. And if she is hesitant to use merit as her criterion, she has only two alternatives: either she must hire enough staff to allow everyone flex time, or she must give all employees equal access to it by devising some sort of rotation schedule, which would necessitate limiting any single employee's right to flex time to, say, a year.

The main point is parity—an acknowledgment that childless employees have as much right to their personal lives as working parents do. And if Jessica doesn't strive toward such equality at ClarityBase, then she had better be prepared to spend months searching for replacements for both Davis and Jana, replacements who are willing to be treated as second-class employees.

STEWART D. FRIEDMAN *is the director of Ford's Leadership Development Center in Dearborn, Michigan. He is on leave from the University of Pennsylvania's Wharton School of Business, where he directs the Work/Life Integration Project. He recently published, with Jeff Greenhaus,* Work and Family—Allies or Enemies? *(Oxford, 2000).*

The goal is equity, not equality. Everyone's life outside of work should be treated with respect, but not necessarily identically. Jessica needs to embrace her employees' diversity by supporting their different passions. If she makes an effort to meet the personal-life needs of each individual on her staff, she will increase the vitality and commitment of her department.

The key is flexibility, which has to run both ways, from organization to employee and vice versa. To encourage this two-way flow, Jessica should let her staff know what the dilemmas are and work with them to find solutions. Jessica should meet with each of the eight account managers individually and say, "I want to create an environment where we all respect and support one another, in terms of both our business and personal goals. I'd like for us all to talk about our expectations—in all areas of our lives—as a group. Then we can begin to figure out collectively how to meet those expectations in creative ways that benefit all facets of each person: work, home, community, and self."

Jessica must encourage both Jana and Megan to participate in the discussion, touchy as this might be. Jessica might explain to them that if all team members share their personal priorities, then the opportunities for easy fixes or for leveraging complementary or synergistic interests increase, for the benefit of all. "For example," Jessica might say, "if you were writing a novel in your spare time and Davis were having trouble with his customer Blackhill and Hansen Publishing, you might switch clients with him so that you could develop editorial contacts at B&H." The subtext here, and the main message to her team, is, "We're all in this together."

To arrive at win-win solutions, Jessica and her team must recognize and discuss the demands of the business as well as life outside ClarityBase. This is the essence of what I call "total leadership," which integrates work, home, community, and self. Because ClarityBase has only valued the personal life goals linked to parenthood, there's a legitimate sense of resentment among those without kids at the company. All the more reason for each individual to express what's most important to him or her and for Jessica to encourage employees to recognize, respect, and support those priorities.

This discussion is the tricky part, but it's also where the real breakthroughs occur. People must be encouraged to assume that there are opportunities for achieving their goals in different ways—inside and outside of work—so they don't take a rigid position of, say, "I have to have Thursday mornings off." If employees state their expectations without asserting fixed positions or demands, the dialogue will take off from there.

In looking for creative solutions, Jessica and her team should consider different ways to satisfy customers, especially through the use of technology. Some clients might accept—even welcome—more e-mail and voice mail communications to cut down on the need for face-to-face meetings.

And to ensure that individuals are treated equitably, the team must consider whether certain account managers should receive higher compensation for handling more demanding clients. Perhaps each customer should have a degree-of-difficulty rating. With such a system, some account managers might even prefer difficult clients because of the higher compensation.

That's where Ed, the call-center supervisor, went wrong in scheduling his staff for Labor Day. He made assumptions about what people wanted without establishing a dialogue about what was most important to them. For all he knew, some people might have preferred working on holidays, especially if they would be paid extra for it.

Bill in HR uses the word "accommodate," implying a traditional, zero-sum approach to the connection between work and personal life. Jessica should instead look for synergies across the different domains of her staff's lives. By doing so, she might better tap into their passions and gain the benefits of total leadership: better business results and enriched lives.

Originally published in March 2001
Reprint R0103A

The Truth About Mentoring Minorities

Race Matters

DAVID A. THOMAS

Executive Summary

DIVERSITY HAS BECOME a top priority in corporate America. Despite corporations' best intentions, however, many have failed to achieve a racial mix at the top levels of management. Some have revolving doors for talented minorities, recruiting the best and brightest, only to see them leave, frustrated by their experiences. Others are able to retain high-potential professionals of color but find them mired in middle management.

To understand the different career trajectories of whites and minorities, David Thomas studied the progression of racial minorities at three large U.S. corporations. Here, he explains the three career stages that all professionals advance through, and he discusses why promising white professionals tend to enter fast tracks early in their careers, whereas high-potential minorities typically take off after they have reached middle management.

117

Thomas's research shows that minorities who advance the furthest share one characteristic: a strong network of mentors and corporate sponsors. He found that minorities who plateaued in middle management received mentoring that was basically instructional; it helped them to develop skills. By contrast, minorities who became executives enjoyed fuller developmental relationships with their mentors.

Thomas explains the types of support mentors provide for their protégés and outlines the challenges of mentoring across racial lines. Specifically, he addresses negative stereotypes, public scrutiny, difficulty with role modeling, and peer resentment.

Finally, Thomas challenges the notion that the job of mentors begins and ends with their one-on-one relationships with their protégés. He offers concrete advice on how mentors can support broader initiatives at their organizations to create and enhance conditions that foster the upward mobility of professionals of color.

DIVERSITY HAS BECOME a top priority in corporate America. Despite the best intentions, though, many organizations have failed to achieve racial balance within their executive teams. Some have revolving doors for talented minorities, recruiting the best and brightest only to see them leave, frustrated and even angered by the barriers they encounter. Other companies are able to retain high-potential professionals of color only to have them become mired in middle management. Still others have minorities in their executive ranks, but only in racialized positions, such as those dealing with community relations, equal employment opportunity, or ethnic markets.

In my research on the career progression of minorities at U.S. corporations, I have found that whites and minorities follow distinct patterns of advancement. Specifically, promising white professionals tend to enter a fast track early in their careers, whereas high-potential minorities take off much later, typically after they have reached middle management. I've also found that the people of color who advance the furthest all share one characteristic—a strong network of mentors and corporate sponsors who nurture their professional development.

These findings have key implications for mentors—mainly that to be effective, they must fully appreciate all the developmental roles they play (such as that of coach, advocate, and counselor) and understand the importance of each at different stages of their protégé's career. The mentor of a professional of color must also be aware of the challenges race can present to his protégé's career development and advancement. Only then can the mentor help his protégé build a network of relationships with people who can pave the way to the executive level. As a foundation, then, mentors must first understand how people of color tend to climb the corporate ladder.

Patterns of Movement

In a three-year research project, I studied the career trajectories of minority and white professionals at three major U.S. corporations. The story of one of the participants—Stephen Williams—sheds light on many of the differences in career advancement between whites and minorities. (In the interest of privacy, I have used pseudonyms for the participants. For additional details about the study, see "About the Research" at the end of this article.)

Williams, an African-American, was born and raised in a middle-class neighborhood in Washington, DC. After earning his bachelor's degree at one of the nation's leading colleges, he began his career as a design engineer at a multibillion-dollar electronics corporation. On his first day in the lab there, he encountered a large banner that read, "George Wallace for President." That proclamation for the pro-segregationist former governor of Alabama was an omen of the uphill battle Williams faced. And yet Williams eventually reached the executive level at his organization. Why did he make it when so many other minorities plateaued in middle management?

First, Williams had the good fortune to be hired by Nathan Barrett, a white manager who continually expanded Williams's responsibilities and advised him on office politics. By the end of his early career, Williams had won additional supporters within the company, including Barrett's boss and several white peers who, when they were promoted to management before Williams, vouched for him with their colleagues and recruited him for plum assignments.

Although it took Williams longer to reach middle management than he thought it should, he avoided becoming cynical even as his white peers were being promoted. Instead, he concentrated on strengthening his technical proficiency, taking numerous in-house courses and seminars. He also chose his assignments judiciously, consciously avoiding being sidetracked into nontechnical or support jobs. Throughout this period, he earned the reputation for being an excellent performer, and he gained the cooperation, respect, and sometimes the friendship of whites who were initially either resistant or hesitant to work with him. After seven years as an engineer, Williams decided to pursue his MBA while continuing to work in engineering and design assignments. The education facilitated his transition into management when he was finally promoted two years later.

Once in middle management, Williams's career took off; he was charged with coordinating the engineering, manufacturing, and field service for ensuring the quality of what was to become a major product family. His success in that position propelled him to a series of other assignments, including a temporary one in strategic planning, that eventually landed him a promotion to vice president and general manager, with profit-and-loss responsibility for a major business unit.

Williams's experiences were typical of the minority executives in my study, which tracked the various stages of career development. Stage 1 covered entry level to middle management. Stage 2 included middle management to upper middle management. (A person in Stage 2 supervised other managers and had responsibility for a functional department within a business unit—for example, the director of marketing or a plant manager.) And Stage 3 covered upper middle management to the executive level. (A person in this stage became a corporate officer or a direct report of a corporate officer, with responsibility for an integrated business unit—a division president, for instance—or leadership of a corporate function—such as a vice president of purchasing.)

The most striking aspect of my findings was the consistency of the data. (See the exhibit "Separate and Unequal.") White professionals who eventually became executives—a group I'll henceforth refer to simply as "white executives"—usually entered a fast track in Stage 1, whereas both white and minority professionals who later plateaued in middle management and minorities who eventually became executives all inched along during that period. In Stages 2 and 3, the careers of minorities who ultimately became executives took off, surpassing those of the plateaued managers. This stark difference in the career trajectories of white and minority executives suggests that companies implicitly have two distinct tournaments for access to the top jobs. In the tournament for whites, contenders are sorted early on, and only those deemed most promising proceed to future competition. In the tournament for minorities, the screening process for the best jobs occurs much later. This and other differences have important implications for minority professionals—and for the people mentoring them through the different stages.

Stage 1

According to my research, a pernicious result of the two-tournament system was that many high-potential minorities became discouraged when they failed to be fast-tracked early in their careers. They became demotivated—especially when they saw their white colleagues receive plum assignments and promotions—and de-skilled. As a result, their performance fell to a level that matched their modest rewards.

Minorities in the study who became executives evaluated themselves in terms of personal growth, not external rewards.

But some minorities—those who eventually became executives—avoided that fate. What kept them motivated and prepared to take advantage of opportunities that arrived belatedly? A common thread among them was their relationships with mentors. Even though the minority executives were not on an obvious fast track, influential mentors were investing in them as if they were, which helped prevent them from either ratcheting down their performance or simply leaving the organization.

This is not to say that the minorities in the study who became executives didn't experience their share of disappointments; they did. But they evaluated themselves in terms of personal growth, not external rewards. Committed to excellence, they found the process of learning new skills rewarding. Like Williams, many of them went to graduate school or took training courses to enhance their knowledge. In general, minority executives made

---

Separate and Unequal

White and minority executives do not progress up the corporate ladder in the same way. Early in their careers, high-potential whites enter a fast track, arriving in middle management well before their peers. Promising professionals of color, on the other hand, break through much later, usually after their arrival in middle management. These data are for a multibillion-dollar manufacturer of commodity products; studies at two other large U.S. corporations have shown similar results.

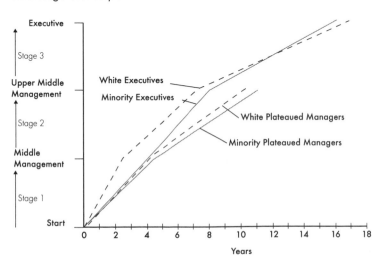

early career choices that placed them at the leading edge of the work they liked. They were more enthusiastic about the work itself and less concerned with how quickly—or slowly—they were climbing the corporate ladder. In fact, two minority executives in the study actually took demotions to transfer from staff jobs into operations, where they saw a better match for their skills and a greater opportunity for professional growth. Stage 1 was thus a time for minority executives to gain the three C's: confidence, competence, and credibility.

In contrast, minority professionals who subsequently plateaued in middle management tended to make their decisions based on perceived fast-track career opportunities, not on the actual work. They were more prone to take salary and title promotions that offered little increase in management responsibility.

Consider the career of Roosevelt James, a minority electrical engineer at the same company as Stephen Williams. While Williams was focused on engineering and design early in his career, James was motivated more by the prospect of getting into management. He took one transfer after another, accepting nominal promotions, believing they were stepping stones to a larger goal. Before reaching middle management, he had had a total of 12 different assignments (nearly all lateral moves) in seven different functional areas, including those in facilities management and affirmative action. Ironically, to fulfill their ambitions for upward mobility, professionals like James sometimes left the path that might have led to the executive suite.

Interestingly, minority executives were promoted to middle management only slightly faster than minority plateaued managers, but with much greater job continuity. They were much less likely to have changed departments, made lateral moves, or transferred away from core positions. Surprisingly, they even received, on average, fewer promotions within a given level than did minorities who failed to make it past middle management. A close inspection of the data, however, revealed that the promotions of minority managers like James offered little real expansion of responsibilities, as compared with the promotions of minority executives like Williams.

Minority executives attributed much of their later success to their immediate bosses, other superiors, and peers who helped them develop professionally. Of course, such developmental relationships are important for everybody climbing the corporate ladder, regardless of race, but what distinguished minority executives from white executives and plateaued managers was that they had many more such relationships and with a broader range of people, especially in the early years of their careers. Within the first three years at the organization, minority executives had established at least one developmental relationship, usually with a boss or a boss's boss. These mentors provided critical support in five ways.

First, the relationships opened the door to challenging assignments that allowed the minority executives to gain professional competence. Second, by putting the future executives in high-trust positions, the mentors sent a message to the rest of the organization that these people were high performers, thus helping them to gain confidence and establish their credibility. Third, the mentors provided crucial career advice and counsel that prevented their protégés from getting sidetracked from the path leading to the executive level. Fourth, the mentors often became powerful sponsors later in the minority executives' careers, recruiting them repeatedly to new positions. Fifth, the mentors often protected their protégés by confronting subordinates or peers who leveled unfair criticism, especially if it had racial undertones. For example, a superior-performing African-American in the study had a laid-back style that detractors said was an indication of his slacking off, playing on the stereotype that blacks are lazy. The mentor directly challenged the detractors by pointing out that his protégé was the leading salesperson in the division.

Such rich mentoring relationships enabled minority executives to build on the three C's, despite temptations to become discouraged. It took Williams, for instance, nine years to reach middle management, whereas it took his white counterparts roughly five. In contrast, professionals of color who plateaued in middle management tended to have circumscribed relationships with their mentors, often limited to work-related issues.

In summary, in Stage 1, the winners in the white tournament earned fast promotions into middle management. In the minority tournament, the signals sent to winners were more subtle, taking the form of rich mentoring relationships, challenging assignments, and expanded responsibilities, which showed the rest of the organization that these people merited future investment. (Winners of the white tournament also received those benefits, but the most obvious prizes in that contest were fast promotions.)

Stage 2

Once minority executives entered middle management, they typically had to wait another ten to 15 years before reaching the executive level. But Stage 2 was usually where their careers took off. And without exception, the minority executives in the study vividly recalled that their initial middle-management jobs were critical to their eventual success. Interestingly, few of the white executives felt that way, perhaps because they didn't regard their jobs in early Stage 2 as big opportunities to prove themselves in the same way that their minority counterparts did.

In Stage 2, minority executives continued to increase their functional knowledge, allowing them to deepen and broaden their foundation of the three C's. When leading others, the sheer technical or functional competence they had acquired in Stage 1 often enabled them to influence subordinates who might otherwise have been resistant. Through that process, they were able to enhance their managerial skills and judgment.

Stage 2 was also an important period for the minority executives to apply their existing skills to complex situations, which then helped them to demonstrate their potential and extend their credibility within the larger organization. Because of that, they were able to expand their network of relationships, including those with mentors and sponsors, beyond the boundaries of their original functional groups. Williams, for example, received several assignments in Stage 2 that required him to develop working relationships with key people in other functional areas. By the end of Stage 2, every minority executive in the study had at least one influential executive as a mentor, and many were highly regarded by several executives who acted as sponsors.

The split between minority executives and plateaued managers became more pronounced in Stage 2. Minority executives still received fewer promotions than minority plateaued managers, but they reached upper middle management in less time because their promotions were bigger and more significant. The assignment patterns of the minority managers continued to be unfocused: they had more job changes—either by department, location, or function (especially changes from line to staff jobs)—and they tended to serve in fix-it roles involving

Stage 2 can be thought of as a catching up and breaking-out period for minority executives.

the same kind of challenges over and over, with no opportunity to acquire new skills.

The career of Carlos Amado, one of the managers studied, is a case in point. By the end of Stage 1, Amado had acquired a deep expertise in manufacturing. He had also earned a reputation for turning around problem groups and making them into stars. But in Stage 2, he failed to learn other important skills, such as developing the supervisors who reported to him and delegating work, and his career subsequently stagnated. A lack of savvy mentoring probably contributed to Amado's incomplete understanding that he was being boxed into a limited role.

Stage 2 was also when the careers of minority and white executives began to converge—their experiences, assignments, and pace of advancement became increasingly similar. There were still, however, some notable differences. Compared with their white counterparts, minority executives were twice as likely to change functions, twice as likely to take on special projects or task force assignments, three times as likely to take a turnaround assignment, almost twice as likely to change locations, and four times as likely to report a big success. In many ways, these differences are a reversal of what occurred in Stage 1, where white executives had markedly more opportunities to prove themselves than minority executives did. For that reason, Stage 2 can be thought of as a catching-up and breaking-out period for minority executives.

Interestingly, although minority and white executives had a similar number of developmental relationships in Stage 2, minority executives were far more likely to have powerful corporate-level executives as sponsors and mentors. In reviewing their careers, minority executives usually described a senior person who had been watching their progress during this period without their full awareness.

Stage 3

The climb from upper middle management to the executive level required a broad base of experience—well beyond a functional expertise. In Stage 3, people took on issues specific to working across functional boundaries, and that change encouraged them to think and act more strategically and politically.

To distinguish oneself as executive-level material in Stage 3, an individual needed highly visible successes that were directly related to the company's core strategy. For Stephen Williams, it was his critical role in developing and launching a product line that helped to reposition his company in the marketplace.

Minority executives in Stage 3 continued developing their network of highly placed mentors and sponsors. An individual's relationship with his executive boss, in particular, became crucial; it played a central role in helping each minority executive break through to the highest level. Furthermore, in Stage 3 the minority executives reported developing at least two new relationships with other executives. In contrast, most of the minority

plateaued managers did not establish any new developmental relationships during that time.

The networks of minority executives were also much
more diverse than those of the minority managers. For
example, African-American managers who plateaued
either relied almost exclusively on members of their own
racial group for key developmental support or they relied
predominantly on whites. In contrast, those who reached
the executive level, especially the most successful among
them, had built genuine, personal long-term relationships with both whites and African-Americans.

The careers of minority and white executives continued to converge in Stage 3, especially with regard to developmental relationships. Clearly, it was impossible to
make it to the executive level, regardless of race, without
the active advocacy of an immediate boss and at least one
other key sponsor or mentor. Nevertheless, as was the
case in Stage 2, minority executives tended to have a
higher proportion of their developmental relationships
with the corporate elite than did white executives.

In summary, during Stages 2 and 3, the careers of
minority executives became clearly differentiated from
that of plateaued managers, and in Stage 3, the career
trajectories and experiences of minority and white executives finally converged.

Mentoring Challenges

A key finding of this research is that professionals of
color who plateaued in management received mentoring
that was basically instructional; it helped them develop
better skills. Minority executives, by contrast, enjoyed
closer, fuller developmental relationships with their

mentors. This was particularly true in people's early careers, when they needed to build confidence, credibility, and competence. That is, purely instructional mentoring was not sufficient; protégés needed to feel connected to their mentors.

Specifically, a mentor must play the dual role of coach and counselor: coaches give technical advice—explaining how to do something—while counselors talk about the experience of doing it and offer emotional support. Both are crucial. If a protégé doesn't have someone to talk to about his experiences in the organization, he will often have trouble implementing any coaching advice. This is especially true early in a person's career, when the instructional advice requires him to assume behaviors that he is not yet comfortable with. Later in the protégé's career, particularly in Stages 2 and 3, the mentor must focus on establishing and expanding a network of relationships, including sponsorship and connections to people who are higher in the organization. While the quality of the interpersonal relationships remains important, the diversity of the network becomes another crucial factor.

Many people, however, do not approach mentoring from a developmental perspective. They don't understand how to work with subordinates, especially minorities, to prepare them for future opportunities. My own experience and the findings of other studies suggest that organizations can change this by educating managers about their developmental role and by teaching them how to mentor effectively. Of prime importance is an understanding of the kinds of developmental relationships that people need at different points in their careers. Also crucial is an appreciation that, because race and racism can pose significant obstacles for people of color, mentors of minorities may need to approach mentoring differently than they do with their white protégés.

CROSS-RACE ISSUES

This education process must include an awareness of the inherent difficulties of mentoring across race. A significant amount of research shows that cross-race (as well as cross-gender) relationships can have difficulty forming, developing, and maturing. Nevertheless, the mentoring of minority professionals must often be across race, as it was for most of the minority executives in my study. And to develop the personal connections that are the foundation of a good mentoring relationship, the participants must overcome the following potential obstacles.

Negative Stereotypes. Mentors must be willing to give their protégés the benefit of the doubt: they invest in their protégés because they expect them to succeed. But a potential mentor who holds negative stereotypes about an individual, perhaps based on race, might withhold that support until the prospective protégé has proven herself worthy of investment. (Such subtle racism may help explain why none of the minority professionals in my study had been fast-tracked. Whites were placed on the fast track based on their perceived potential, whereas people of color had to display a proven and sustained record of solid performance—in effect, they often had to be overprepared—before they were placed on the executive track.)

On the other hand, when a person of color feels that he won't be given the benefit of the doubt, he behaves in certain ways—for example, he might not take risks he should for fear that if he fails, he will be punished disproportionately.

Identification and Role Modeling. Close mentoring relationships are much more likely to form when both parties see parts of themselves in the other person: the protégé sees someone whom he wants to be like in the future. The mentor sees someone who reminds him of himself years ago. This identification process can help the mentor see beyond a protégé's rough edges. But if the mentor has trouble identifying with his protégé—and sometimes differences in race are an obstacle—then he might not be able to see beyond the protégé's weaknesses. Furthermore, when the mentoring relationship is across race, the mentor will often have certain limitations as a role model. That is, if the protégé adopts the behavior of the mentor, it might produce different results. In my study, an African-American participant recounted how his white mentor encouraged him to adopt the mentor's more aggressive style. But when the protégé did so, others labeled him an "angry black man."

Skepticism About Intimacy. At companies without a solid track history of diversity, people might question whether close, high-quality relationships across race are possible. Does the mentor, for example, have an ulterior motive, or is the protégé selling out his culture?

Public Scrutiny. Because cross-race relationships are rare in most organizations, they tend to be more noticeable, so people focus on them. The possibility of such scrutiny will often discourage people from participating in a cross-race relationship in the first place.

Peer Resentment. A protégé's peers can easily become jealous, prompting them to suggest or imply that the protégé does not deserve whatever benefits he's received. Someone who fears such resentment might avoid forming a close relationship with a prospective mentor of another race. Of course, peer resentment occurs even with same-race mentorships, but it is a much greater concern in cross-race relationships because of their rarity.

Such obstacles often hinder cross-race mentoring from reaching its full potential. In my research, I have found that they make people less willing to open up about sensitive issues and more afraid of disagreements and confrontations. The general sense is that cross-race relationships are more fragile.

Not surprisingly, many cross-race mentoring relationships suffer from "protective hesitation": both parties refrain from raising touchy issues. For example, Richard Davis, a white mentor in my study, thought that his African-American protégé's style was abrasive, but he kept that feeling to himself in order to avoid any suggestion that he was prejudiced—specifically that he harbored the stereotype that all black men are brash and unpolished. Davis eventually found out that he was right when his protégé's style became an issue with others. At that point, though, his protégé was deemed to have a problem—one that could have been prevented had Davis only spoken sooner.

Many cross-race mentoring relationships suffer from "protective hesitation": both parties refrain from raising touchy issues.

Protective hesitation can become acute when the issue is race—a taboo topic for many mentors and protégés. People believe that they aren't supposed to talk about race; if they have to discuss it, then it must be a problem. But that mind-set can cripple a relationship. Consider, for example, a protégé who thinks that a client is giving him a difficult time because of his race but keeps his opinion to himself for fear that his mentor will think he has a chip on his shoulder. Had the protégé raised the issue, his mentor might have been able to nip the problem early on. The mentor, for instance, might have sent the protégé to important client meetings alone, thereby signaling that the protégé has the backing of his mentor and the authority to make high-level decisions.

The above example highlights an important finding from my research: minorities tend to advance further when their white mentors understand and acknowledge race as a potential barrier. Then they can help their protégés deal effectively with some of those obstacles. In other words, relationships in which protégé and mentor openly discuss racial issues generally translate into greater opportunity for the protégé.

To encourage and foster that type of mentoring, organizations can teach people, especially managers, how to identify and surmount various race-related difficulties. For example, a white mentor might make a concerted effort to communicate to her minority protégé that she has already given him the benefit of the doubt. In a meeting, she could openly endorse his good ideas, thereby signaling to others that they, too, should value his opinions. Such actions would curb the protégé's fear of failure and encourage him to take risks and speak about difficulties.

And consider the practice of role modeling. If a mentor accepts that he might be limited in his ability to serve as a role model, he can help his protégé identify other appropriate people. He can also offer open-ended advice, perhaps by using qualifying comments ("This might not work for you, but from my experience...") and invite discussion of the advice rather than assume it will be taken. Otherwise, the mentor might easily misconstrue situations when his advice isn't taken, which could make the mentor feel slighted and possibly even cause him to abandon the relationship.

It should be noted that when the complexities of cross-race relationships are handled well, they can strengthen a relationship. For one thing, if a mentor and protégé trust each other enough to work together in dealing with touchy race-related issues, then they will likely have a sturdy foundation to handle other problems. In fact, people have reported that race differences enabled them to explore other kinds of differences, thus broadening the perspectives of both parties. That education was invaluable because people who can fully appreciate the uniqueness of each individual are more likely to be better managers and leaders. Indeed, in my research on cross-race mentoring, mentors have frequently reported those relationships were the most fulfilling in terms of their own growth and transformation.

NETWORK MANAGEMENT

As discussed earlier, one of a mentor's key tasks is to help the protégé build a large and diverse network of relationships. The network must be strong enough to withstand even the loss of the mentor. Stephen Williams's mentor, for example, left the company after Williams had entered Stage 3 and was tackling increasingly challenging assignments.

From my research, I have found that the most effective network is heterogeneous along three dimensions. First, the network should have functional diversity; it should include mentors, sponsors, role models, peers, and even people whom the protégés themselves might be developing mentoring relationships toward. Second, the network should have variety with respect to position (seniors, colleagues, and juniors) as well as location (people within the immediate department, in other departments, and outside the organization). And third, the network should be demographically mixed in terms of race, gender, age, and culture.

Although a detailed description of the three dimensions is beyond the scope of this article, several points are worth noting. The difference between mentorship and sponsorship is that the former entails a much closer personal connection. Sponsors are coaches and advocates, whereas mentors are also counselors, friends, and in many ways surrogate family. Nevertheless, the role of sponsors can be critical when, for example, the protégé wants to pursue an opportunity outside the mentor's department. Also, especially when key decisions at an organization are made by committee, the protégé will benefit from having as many sponsors as possible.

A frequently overlooked area is a protégé's relationships with peers. People of color, in particular, can oftentimes become isolated from their peers due to resentment. But peer networks are crucial. For one thing, peers can help one another manage their careers and perform important self-assessments. They can be sympathetic sounding boards, useful information checks (what was your experience like when you first started in that division?), and helpful devil's advocates. For Stephen Williams, participation in a self-help group of African-Americans at his organization provided valuable social support and also expanded his network beyond his association with his engineering colleagues.

To ensure that a protégé is not missing any important peer relationships, the mentor must sometimes intervene. For example, if a mentor notices that his protégé is not part of an informal go-to-lunch crowd, he might assign her to a certain project with people in that group to encourage those friendships to form.

Another often overlooked area is a protégé's relationships with juniors, which will help the protégé become a valuable mentor in the future. Also, particularly for people in middle management, good relationships with junior staff can enable them to stay up-to-date with the latest technology. Furthermore, a protégé's mentors and superiors can be influenced greatly by the opinions of junior staff.

A network of relationships becomes vulnerable when it lacks any one of the dimensions. For example, if a person's network is limited to his organization, he will find it difficult to find employment elsewhere. On the other hand, people of color have the tendency to draw on a network from primarily outside their organizations. Such support can be invaluable, but it will provide little help when that individual is being considered for a highly desirable in-house assignment. Establishing a diverse network is just the start—a person's network must be replenished and modified continually.

Creating the Environment for Success

Many mentors of minority professionals assume that their job begins and ends with the one-on-one relationships they establish with their protégés. This is hardly true. Mentors, especially those at the executive level, must do much more by actively supporting broader efforts and initiatives at their organizations to help create the conditions that foster the upward mobility of people of color. Specifically, they can do the following:

- Ensure that the pool of people being considered for promotions and key assignments reflects the diversity in the organization.

- Promote executive development workshops and seminars that address racial issues.

- Support in-house minority associations, including networking groups.

- Help colleagues manage their discomfort with race. In a meeting to decide whether someone of color should be promoted, for example, a person can help focus the discussion on the individual's actual performance while discounting racial issues disguised as legitimate concerns (such as vague criticisms that the managerial style of the minority candidate "doesn't fit in").

- Challenge implicit rules, such as those that assume that people who weren't fast movers early in their careers will never rise to the executive suites.

In conclusion, I should address one of the most insidious implicit rules of all: the two-tournament model. Many companies might be tempted to accept it as an empirical reality. Some might even want to make it policy by tacitly accepting that minorities cannot be fast-tracked in their early careers or by formally creating two separate career tournaments—one for whites and one for minorities. They assume that minorities will move more slowly in Stage 1. So, the thinking goes, why not take that time to ensure that high-potential minorities are overprepared to meet the social, technical, and racial challenges when they reach Stage 2?

I believe that any acceptance—let alone conscious replication—of the two-tournament system is a mistake. First, it unfairly institutionalizes the "tax" of added time that minorities have to pay as a result of existing racial barriers. As a consequence, a higher standard is set for their participation in the main competition for executive jobs. Second, such a policy would likely result in a number of high-performing and ambitious minorities leaving in Stage 1, before their careers could accelerate. It was beyond the scope of my study to determine exactly how many people of color with executive potential left during Stage 1, but I did encounter many executives who were surprised when their best minority talent left "just as good things were about to happen." Lastly, a two-tournament model could eventually lead to backlash among white plateaued managers who, not realizing that they had been passed over in Stage 1 because they were not deemed executive material, become resentful toward the promising minorities taking off in Stages 2 and 3.

Organizations should provide a range of career paths, uncorrelated with race, that lead to the executive suite.

But I am not advocating a one-tournament system of fast-tracking. After all, it is no accident that people of color haven't been fast-tracked in the past. One reason is that organizations have been largely ineffective in helping minorities establish relationships with mentors. Thus, artificially placing minority professionals onto a fast track without first changing the underlying process dynamics would set up those individuals for failure.

Organizations instead should provide a range of career paths, all uncorrelated with race, that lead to the executive suite. Ideally, this system of movement would allow variation across all groups—people could move at their own speed through the three stages based on their individual strengths and needs, not their race. Achieving this system, however, would require integrating the principles of opportunity, development, and diversity into the fabric of the organization's management practices and human resource systems. And an important element in the process would be to identify potential mentors, train them, and ensure that they are paired with promising professionals of color.

About the Research

MY THREE-YEAR RESEARCH PROJECT took place at three major U.S. corporations: a manufacturer of commodity products, an electronics company, and a high-tech firm. At these multibillion-dollar organizations, I conducted in-depth case studies of 20 minority executives, predominantly African-Americans but also Asian- and Hispanic-Americans. For comparison purposes, I also conducted in-depth studies of 13 white executives as well as 21 nonexecutives (people who had plateaued in middle management), both white and minority, from the same companies. In addition, I reviewed the promotion records of more than 500 managers and executives at one of the companies studied.

Each corporation in the study had a long history of commitment to diversity. Amid the civil rights environment of the 1960s and early 1970s, all had strongly supported both affirmative action and equal employment opportunities. Their civic and community involvement helped their initial efforts to recruit minorities for professional and managerial positions. By the early 1990s, these companies had achieved racial integration within their management ranks.

Some people have questioned my decision to study only companies with a good track record in terms of diversity. The reason is simple: I felt that these companies would have more to teach us about how minority executives could succeed—even given various obstacles. I do not, however, mean to gloss over the very real—and sometimes insurmountable—barriers that many nonwhites face in their quest for advancement in corporate America. Indeed, there are still many companies at which no amount of individual effort, preparation, or performance is likely to propel a person of color into an executive position.

Originally published in April 2001
Reprint R0104F

Two Women, Three Men on a Raft

ROBERT SCHRANK

Executive Summary

THE OUTWARD BOUND raft trip in 1977 was meant to build better teamwork and teach the art and techniques of survival under difficult conditions. All 20 participants were successful executives in their mid-50s. But Raft No. 4 was the only one on the trip with a mix of men and women.

Over the week that followed, the five people on Raft No. 4 created a supportive atmosphere, sharing some jobs and informally assigning others according to preference and inclination. The men did most of the heavy work, while the women cleaned the ground and arranged the sleeping bags. Everyone was required to take a turn at the helm, a challenge that the men embraced but that the women tried to avoid and then carried out badly. On the fifth day, with one of the women at the rudder, the raft overturned in a rapids. The dunking was a narrow escape for them all, and from then on, only men took the helm.

It was only when the trip was over that the author began to realize what really lay behind Raft No. 4's accident. In fact, the men had unconsciously worked together to hold on to their power, building on the women's individual doubts about their own capacities for leadership. The men supported each other at the helm, but they wanted to see the women fail and conspired tacitly to bring about their failure. The author draws the inescapable parallels with the gender rivalries that keep women from rising to positions of power within organizations.

The author and three women—including one of the two women on Raft No. 4—comment on whether and how circumstances have changed since HBR first published this article 17 years ago.

ONE AFTERNOON IN JUNE, I left the cloistered halls of the Ford Foundation and within 36 hours found myself standing on the banks of the Rogue River in Oregon with three other uncertain souls who had embarked on a week of "survival training" sponsored by Outward Bound. It was a cloudy, cold day, and as we pumped up our rubber raft and contemplated the Rogue, we also wondered about one another. Before embarking on a Greyhound for the raft launching site, we had gathered the night before at the Medford Holiday Inn. That night, the Outward Bound staff had distributed individual camping gear and waterproof sleeping/storage bags to the 20 of us, almost all novices, and had given us a short briefing on the perils of going down the Rogue River on a raft.

As they explained the nature of the trip, the Outward Bound staffers reminded me of seasoned military men or safari leaders about to take a group of know-nothings into a world of lurking danger. Their talk was a kind of machismo jargon about swells, rattlers, safety lines, portages, and pitons. Because they had known and conquered the dangers, it seemed they could talk of such things with assurance. This kind of "man talk" called to a primitive ear in us novices, and we began to perceive the grave dangers out there as evils to be overcome. In our minds, we were planning to meet "Big Foot" the very next day, and we were secretly thrilled at the prospect.

If the Outward Bound staff briefing was designed to put us at ease, its effect, if anything, was the opposite. Hearing the detailed outline of what would be expected of us increased our anxiety. "You will work in teams as assigned to your raft," said Bill Boyd, the Northwest Outward Bound director, "and you will be responsible for running your raft, setting up camp each night, cooking every fourth meal for the whole gang, and taking care of all your own personal needs."

The staff divided the 20 of us into four groups, each of which would remain together for the week on the raft. How we were grouped was never explained to us, but of the five rafts on the river, our raft, No. 4, was the only one that ended up with two women and three men. One of the men was a member of the Outward Bound staff, a counselor and guide who was considerably younger than his four charges.

The staff used a lot of machismo jargon but told us little about what we might actually expect.

The four of us on Raft No. 4 were all in our middle fifties. Each of us had experienced some modicum of success in his or her life, and Outward Bound had invited each of us in the hope that after a week of living on the Rogue River we would go back from the trip as Outward Bound supporters and promoters.

On the River

Like most of the other 19 people on the trip, at the outset I had little or no idea of what to expect. I had participated in a few human growth encounter workshops, so I was prepared for, although again surprised at, how willingly people seem to accept the authority of a completely unknown group leader. Most people seem able to participate in all kinds of strange and, in many instances, new behaviors with no knowledge regarding the possible outcomes. This group was no exception. All of us had some notion of Outward Bound, but we knew nothing about each other, or our raft leader John, or the Rogue River.

Even though their preembarkation talk was filled with the machismo jargon I mentioned, the staff did not describe what we might actually expect to happen, nor did they talk about the many other river trips they had been on. I suppose the staff leaders assumed that the best way for a group of people to learn about themselves and each other is to let the experience talk to them directly.

The two women assigned to Raft No. 4 were named Marlene and Helen. Marlene was a recently divorced mother of five kids from Washington, whom a number of us had observed in her pink bikini in the Holiday Inn pool when we had arrived. Most of us acknowledged that because of that build we would love to have her along. Marlene used to wear her red ski suit at night and talked a lot about the good times she'd spent on the ski slopes. A top-notch skier, she said she divorced her husband because she was tired of making believe he was a better skier than she was.

Helen, a big blonde woman with a fierce sense of humor and a divorced mother of two grown boys, was at the time of our trip the president of the Fund Center in Denver, a coordinating body for local foundations, as well as a political activist. She and I became each other's clowns, and one night at a campfire she leaned over and asked me, "Bobby, is this just another plaything of the bored rich, or can we really learn something out here in this God-forsaken wilderness?" I told her I wasn't sure but we ought to give it a chance, which we certainly did.

One of the two other men was Bill, a very successful lawyer from Darien, Connecticut. He was the only one of the four passengers who was still happily married, since I too was divorced. Bill was a busy executive, but he managed to find time for hiking, skiing, and fishing. While Outward Bound took care of all our food requirements and most of our medical needs, Raft No. 4 had its own supply officer in Bill. His backpack was organized like a Civil War surgeon's field kit. He had all his changes of clothing scheduled, and when it rained, his extra plastic rainjacket kept me dry since mine leaked like a sieve. Though he and Marlene were obviously attracted to each other from the start, it was clear from his "happy family" talk that nothing was going to change, and it didn't.

The other man was John Rhoades, our heavily mustached, vigorous leader, in his early thirties, who saw himself as a teacher, educator, and trainer. As a progressive educator, John was overdedicated to the notion that no one can learn from anyone else since learning is a singular, unique experience.

There was a lot of forced joking as we tried to overcome our anxieties.

The men and women of Raft No. 4 were a warm, friendly, outgoing bunch, each of whom helped create a nice, supportive atmosphere.

When we arrived at the river, each was anxious to pitch in and do his or her part. The staff distributed the rafts, each of which had a small foot pump, and Bill and I, with instruction from John, proceeded to inflate ours. It was one of our first chores, and we did it with a machismo fervor that suggested either previous knowledge, or that it was man's work or both. Marlene and Helen carried food bags, buckets, and ropes. It was a cold day, a gray mist hung over the towering Oregon pines, and I had a feeling that at least some of us, given a choice, would have opted for going back to the Holiday Inn. There was a lot of forced joking and kidding, with which we attempted to overcome some of our anxieties—we were whistling in the dark.

John gave each of us a Mae West-type life preserver and instructed us on how to use it. He told us, "You are not to go on the raft without it." Now with all of us bulging out of our Mae Wests, a Richter scale applied to anxiety would have registered eight or a full-scale breakdown. Postponing the inevitable, we shivered, fussed, and helped each other get adjusted to our life jackets. The trip down the Rogue River was beginning to take on a serious quality.

The rafts we used were small, about 10 feet long and 4 feet wide. The passengers sit on the inflated outer tube with their feet on the inside. Everyone is very close together with little or no room to move around. Also, unlike a boat, a raft has no keel or rudder mechanism, which means that it tends to roll and bobble around on top of the water. Unless the occupants work as a team and use their paddles in close coordination, it is very difficult to control.

While we were still on shore, John perched himself in the helms-man position at the back of the raft and said, "OK, I am going to teach you how to navigate the Rogue. When I say 'right turn,' the two people on the left side of the raft are to paddle forward and the two on the right are to backpaddle. When I say 'left turn,' the two people on the right are to paddle forward and the two on the left are to backpaddle. When I say 'forward,' I want everyone digging that paddle in like his life depended on it, and when I say 'backpaddle,' everyone paddle backward. When I say 'hold,' all paddles out of the water. Now, have you all got it, or should we go over it again?" We pushed the raft out over the beach pebbles and paddled out into the Rogue, which at this point seemed like just a nice pond. John barked his commands to us, and the team did just fine in the quiet water.

John told us that we were Raft No. 4 of five rafts, and it was important to everyone's safety that each raft maintain its position so that we could make periodic personnel checks to make sure no one was missing. John gave the command "forward," and because No. 3 raft was already far ahead of us and out of sight, Marlene, Helen, Bill, and I paddled vigorously.

We were each to take a turn at ruddering the raft and issuing commands.

As we proceeded down the river, John announced, "Each of you will take turns at being the helmsman." After some comment by Helen, this term was quickly corrected to conform to the new nondiscriminatory linguistics, as well as for the EEOC, to "helmsperson." John said that this person would be in charge of the raft— steering from the stern and issuing the commands.

As John talked, my mind drifted. I was suddenly overwhelmed by the grandeur and beauty of this great wilderness river road we were traveling. In awe of the hugeness of the trees, I did not hear or respond to a command. John, a very earnest fellow, was somewhat annoyed at my daydreaming and upbraided me, saying, "Look, we all have to concentrate on our job or we will be in trouble." And then he explained the nature of the rapids ahead.

He told us how to recognize a rapid's tongue (entrance), how to avoid "sleepers" (hidden rocks), and then how to ride the "haystacks" (the choppy waves that form at the outlet of the rapids) as you come through the rapids. He said that the most important art we would learn would be how to chop our paddles into the waves as we rode the haystacks. Since a raft has no seat belts, or even seats for that matter, unless you chop down hard, the rough water can bounce you right out of it.

As we paddled through the still calm waters, trying to catch up with Raft No. 3, Helen began to complain that she was already getting tired. "I'm just not used to pushing a paddle, but I'm damn good at pushing a pencil," she said. I, too, was beginning to feel the strain of the paddle, but rather than admit it to anyone, I just laughed saying, "Why this is nothing, Helen. You should canoe the St. John in Maine. That would teach you." Bill chimed in with "Yeah, this is nothing compared to climbing Pike's Peak."

As we moved down the river, a faint distant roar broke the silence of the forest. And as we drew nearer to it, our excitement increased. One might have thought that rather than a four-foot rapids, Niagara Falls lay dead ahead. I was relieved when, some distance before the rapids, John told us to head for the bank where we would go ashore and study the rapids first. As a team we would then decide together what kind of course to take through them.

We had been on the river now for a few hours, and, as it would be many times during the trip, getting on dry land was a great relief. Life on a small rubber raft consists of sitting in ankle-deep cold water, anticipating a periodic refill over both the side of the raft and one's genitals. If there was not time to bail out, we would just sit in the cold water. And even if there were time, we would still be soaking wet and cold from the hips down. Though this was our first chance to escape the cold water treatment, we quickly learned to look forward to such opportunities. The physical discomfort we felt together on the raft was overcoming our sense of being strangers; by the time we disembarked that first time, we were a band of fellow sufferers.

At that point on the river, the bank was very steep, so we had a tough climb up a high rock cliff to get a good look at the rapids. Just before the rapids, the river makes a sharp 90-degree bend creating an additional danger. The swiftly running river could pile the raft up on the bank or into a hidden rock. After considerable discussion, during which Bill and I tried to demonstrate to Helen and Marlene our previous if not superior knowledge of boating, we agreed on taking a left course into the tongue while at the same time trying to bear right to avoid being swept onto the bank.

Coming up and down the steep river bank, Bill helped Marlene over the rocks, holding her elbow. A ways behind them, Helen commented to me, "Honestly, Bob, Marlene isn't that helpless." As we climbed into the raft, Bill helped Marlene again, and I, smiling sheepishly, offered my arm to Helen. I said, holding the raft, "Well, if we go, we all go together, and may we all end up in the same hospital room." Sitting herself down, Helen asked, "Who will notify the next of kin since no one will be left?"

After they were seated, Bill and I huddled and agreed that if anything went wrong, he would look after Marlene and I would look after Helen.

Once back on the river, with John at the helm, we paddled into the rapid's tongue, where the raft picked up speed. Staying to the left but maintaining our right orientation, before we knew what had happened, we were roaring through the tongue, roller coasting through the haystacks, screaming with excitement. Flushed with our first real achievement, the raft awash with ice-cold water, we patted each other on the back for our first great success. While bailing out the raft, we paid each other compliments and convinced ourselves that we could master the Rogue River.

But this was our first set of rapids, and while John assured us that we had done well, he also reminded us of the meaner rapids yet to come with such potent names as Mule Creek Canyon, Blossom Bar, Big Bend, Copper Canyon, and Grave Creek. My God, I thought, did we really have to go through all of those terrible places?

When either woman tried to carry the supplies, Bill yelled, "Hey, hold it. That's too heavy for you."

Life on the Rogue included many other things besides shooting rapids. We pitched tarpaulins every night, lugged supplies in and out of the raft, and became accustomed to the discomforts of having no running water and of being absolutely frozen after sitting in cold water for the whole day. Nothing cements a group together like collective misery, and the people of Raft No. 4 had a real concern for each other as mutually suffering human beings.

Each raft carried a watertight supply bag of sleeping bags and personal clothing. The bag was strapped to the front of the raft and had to be carried to and fro every morning and night. When we tied up at our first camp-site, Marlene and Helen each took an end and started to carry the bag from the raft up the bank. Bill ran after them yelling, "Hey, hold it. That's too heavy for you," and grabbed the bag. Throwing it over his shoulder, he said, "You shouldn't try to do that heavy stuff." Marlene smiled at him and said, "Bill, anytime, be my guest." Helen, who seemed to be a little annoyed, commented sarcastically, "Well it's great to have these big, strong men around now, ain't it though?"

When we came off the raft at night, most everybody instantly undressed to put on dry clothes, caring not one fig for a leaf or modesty. But even though on the surface it looked as though the physical sex differences had disappeared, the emergency nature of things exerted a different pressure, forcing each of us to "do what you know best."

Bill and I, for example, would pitch the tarpaulins each night and haul water, while Marlene and Helen would make the beds, clean the ground, and arrange the sleeping bags. Our mutual concern was evident; it was a beautiful experience of caring for one's fellow sisters and brothers, and I loved it.

After pitching our plastic tarpaulins (which were not much bigger than queen-size beds) as protection against the rain, the four of us would wiggle into our sleeping bags for the night. The first night Helen said she thought we were "four wonderful people gone batty sleeping on the hard cold ground when we could all be in soft feather beds." We laughed and helped each other zip up, arranged sweaters as pillows, and made sure we were all protected. Raft No. 4 was a real team.

During the days, I was beginning to learn some basics about rafts and rapids. Once the raft starts down the river and enters a swiftly moving rapid, the helmsperson must give and the crew respond to commands in quick succession in order to avoid hidden rocks, suck holes, boulders, and other obstacles, which can either flip the raft over or pull it under, bouncing it back like a ball.

As we approached the second rapids, we again went ashore to "look over our approach." It was a bad situation since the rapids planed out over a very rocky riverbed. Helen suggested that we let John take the raft through while we watch. "Now Bob," she said, "do we really care about this damn river? I don't care if we can squeak through these rocks or not. Hit your head on them or something and you could really get hurt." Bill, John, and I cheered us on.

When I became helmsperson, I discovered how difficult it is to steer a raft. The helmsperson can have some effect on the direction of the raft, and because Bill and I had some boating experience, we were at least familiar with the idea of using the paddle as a rudder. Neither Helen nor Marlene seemed to understand how to use a paddle that way, nor did they have the experience.

When one of the two women on our raft—more so Marlene than Helen—was the helmsperson, she would chant, "I can't do it; I can't do it." Each time they cried out, neither Bill nor I would answer right away, but we would eventually try to convince them that they could. Typically, Marlene would say, "I don't know right from left. One of you guys do it; you're so much better."

At Copper Canyon, we needed a "hard right" command. With Marlene at the helm, we got a "hard left" instead. Bill and I looked at each other in utter disgust.

He asked Marlene, "What's the matter, honey?"

She said, "I don't know right from left. You be the helmsperson."

He said, "Why don't we write on the back of your hands the words 'right' and 'left'?"

Bill was kidding, but the next thing I knew, they were doing it.

Helen was mad and said to me, "Is it really necessary to make a baby out of her?"

"No," I answered her, "of course not. But she really doesn't know right from left."

As Marlene would say, "I can't do it," Bill and I would say, "Of course you can do it. It's easy; you're doing just fine." All the time we were speaking, we were thinking, "Ye gods! When is she going to give up?" Each time either Marlene or Helen would be helmsperson, we'd have the same conversation; each time Bill's and my reassurances would be more and more halfhearted. Before long, we weren't responding at all.

As the days wore on, Bill and I proceeded subtly but surely to take charge. The teamwork was unraveling. When we approached a tongue, if either Marlene or Helen were helmsperson, Bill and I would look at each other, and with very slight headshakes and grimaces, we would indicate agreement that things were not going well at all.

Once we had established that things were not going well, we then felt free to take our own corrective measures, such as trying to steer the raft from our forward paddle positions, which turned out to be an almost impossible thing to do. Not only is running the raft from the front not at all helpful to the person at the helm, but also if the helmsperson is not aware of the counterforces, the raft can easily turn around like a carousel. The unaware helmsperson is then totally out of control. Each time that would happen, Marlene would say, "I just don't know what's wrong with me," and Helen would echo her,

"I don't know what's wrong with me either." Bill's and my disgust would mount.

Eventually, John became fed up with the inability of the bunch on Raft No. 4 to work together, which was mainly a result, he said, of the two "captains" in the front. As a last resort, he ordered each one of us to give a single command that he or she would shout as needed. My command was "hold," Bill's command was "left," Marlene's was "right," and Helen's was "backpaddle." John's teaching objective for the group was to get the four of us working together, or else. Needless to say, "or else" prevailed.

On the fifth day, Marlene was helmsperson. Bill and I were in the bow, silently anxious. Even voluble Helen was silent as the raft approached a fast-moving chute. At that time, only a clear, concise, direct command and a rapid response would be of any use at all.

Instead of a "hard right" command, we had no command. Marlene froze, the raft slid up on a big boulder, and in an instant we flipped over like a flapjack on a griddle. The current was swift and swept the five of us away in different directions. As I splashed around in the cold water, cursing that "Goddamned dumb Marlene," I spotted Bill nearby. The two of us began together to look for Marlene and Helen, whom we found each grappling with paddles and gear they'd grabbed as the raft had gone over. We assured each other that we were OK and expressed relief at finding each other.

Cold, wet, and shivering uncontrollably, we made our way out of the river. To warm us and to keep us moving, John chased us around the bank to get wood for a fire. He stuffed us with candies and other sweets to give us energy. As we stood around the fire, chilled and wet, unable to stop shaking, we talked about what had happened, and why.

There was mutiny in the air now, and a consensus emerged. The four of us were furious at John and blamed him for our predicament. John retreated, but finally we were agreed that we would not have any more of this kind of thing. Regardless of John's wishes, anyone who did not want to be helmsperson could simply pass. Marlene was certain that she wanted no part of being at the helm, and Helen, though less sure, was happy to say, "Yeah, I just want to stay dry. I'll let you guys take the helm."

After becoming somewhat dry, sober, and a bit remorseful, the crew of Raft No. 4 returned to the river to resume our run down the Rogue. We had lost our No. 4 position, the other rafts having run past us. John was helmsperson. Helen and Marlene were settled into their backpaddle seats. Bill and I, miffed over our mishap, felt self-conscious and fell silent thinking of the joshing we'd receive from the other rafts.

We slowly overcame the tensions of our crisis, and as the trip came to an end, we were friends again; the fifth day was forgotten. As we climbed out of the raft for the last time, Marlene said, "Well, the next raft trip I take, it will be as a passenger and not as a crew member."

That last night on the Rogue, we celebrated with a big party. The women dressed up in improvised bangles and baubles. I was the maître d', and none of us thought much about what really had happened on Raft No. 4.

Deliverance

What really happened on the river? Why did the raft flip over? Not until I was back in the comfort of my office did I begin to understand, and the realization of the truth was as shocking as any of the splashes of cold water had been on the Rogue. It became clear to me that not only had I been unhappy with a woman as helmsperson, but also that Bill and I had subconsciously, by habit, proceeded to undermine the women. When one of the other two men was in charge, I was comfortable, supportive, and worked to help him be a better helmsperson. When a woman was at the helm, I seemed to direct my activity at getting her replaced rapidly by one of the men.

A most revealing part of the raft experience, however, was not so much the power relationship between the sexes, which I think I understood, but how Bill and I unconsciously or automatically responded to protect our power from female encroachment. When the trip started, I knew that I might have some difficulty accepting a woman at the helm, but I did not realize that the threat would be so great that I would actually desire to see her fail. On that trip I did something new: I actively tried to sabotage Marlene's and Helen's efforts to lead.

Bill and I were unconsciously building on each woman's doubts about herself with negative reinforcement of her leadership role. The effect of our male, sabotaging behavior was to increase Helen's and Marlene's doubts about themselves as leaders. For each of them, their lifelong conditioning that a woman ought to be a passive sweet thing came into play, and eventually both of them gave up the helm because men "do it better."

If the reader thinks males are just threatened in the outdoors, look what happens to us indoors. First, there is the machismo business, which is a cultural way of granting power to males. To the macho male, it is his role to take care of the woman, particularly in the face of imminent danger, and in the course of things, he should never yield any power. In most organizational settings, the male need to be in charge in the presence of females may be subtle, which may make it harder to identify than on a raft on a swift-flowing river. If all the male readers of this article would write down just one way to undermine the budding woman executive, there would be quite a list.

Judging from firsthand experience and reports from other people, I believe that what happened on Raft No. 4, Inc., occurs in most organizations when women enter positions of leadership. An exception might be organizations that have been run by women from their inception. Because organizations are usually designed as pyramids, the moving-up process entails squeezing someone else out. The higher up the pyramid, the more the squeeze. As women enter the squeezing, men are doubly threatened; first, the number of pyramid squeeze players is increasing; second, because the new players are women, our masculinity is on the block. The resentment of men toward women managers is also exacerbated by the realities of a shrunken job market.

As more women become managers in organizations, there will have to be a shift in power. The men who hold that power in fierce competition with each other will not expand the competition by encouraging women to become part of the battle without considerable changes in their own consciousness. In a wilderness setting, all decisions, either one's own or the group's, have immediate consequences, such as being dumped out of the raft, as we saw. The rightness or wrongness of decisions in organizations is not so obvious since they may have no perceptible effects for days or even months. During this time lag, the male unconscious activity can occur to undermine the female.

Will women in administrative positions be supported, ignored, or subconsciously sabotaged by men who find their power threatened? As most experienced administrators know, a major problem in running an organization is directly related to the level of subordinate support. How should the organization go? Straight ahead, hold, turn left, or turn right? These decisions are judgments that may be tough, but the leader must make them; and unless they are supported by the subordinates, they might as well never have been made.

A command of "hard right" can be executed as hard-hard, half-hard, and soft-hard, the last one being equal to just a facade of cooperation. That situation is the most dangerous one for the leader who presumes that orders are being executed, while in fact the raft is foundering. I suspect that one of the reasons that a woman has trouble is because the lack of support she receives from one man gets reinforced by others; it is a collective activity. Things might have been different on Raft No. 4 had we been willing to confront each other. It might have spoiled the fun, but we all might have learned something.

At first, I thought there might not be much of an analogy between navigating a river and a big bureaucracy. Now I think there is. The requirements turn out to be different, and yet the same. The river is more easily understood: how it flows, its hydraulics, its sleepers, or its chutes, and women, like men, can learn these things. A big organization also has sleepers and chutes, but recognizing their existence is a far more political than intellectual task. Women trying to navigate most organizations may find them more complex than the Rogue, but they need to look for similar hazards. The sleepers and chutes will be vested groups of men, who, when their power is threatened, will pull any woman down for tinkering with their interests.

Retrospective Commentaries

ROBERT SCHRANK *reassesses the Rogue River raft trip 17 years later.*

After my trip down the Rogue River 17 years ago, I suspected that more had happened there than I realized at first. Only after an extended period of reflection, however, did my conscious mind grasp what my unconscious had known all along—that during the course of the trip I had effectively conspired with John and Bill to sabotage the performance of Helen and Marlene. In the article, I admitted as much.

Before the article appeared, I showed the manuscript to several people, all men. "Really now, Schrank," the response was, "you're not going to publish that foolishness, are you?" But I did, and then other men asked whether I really believed "that crap you wrote" or whether I hadn't made up "all that stuff about what we do to women." I thought their comments suggested that I had somehow betrayed a male tribal secret.

Women have undoubtedly made progress in the corporate workplace since the article first appeared, but certainly not as much as they had expected. We have new laws, rules, and policies relating to women in the workplace, but what we haven't changed much is the male behavior. Women have fallen short in their goals—of crashing through the glass ceiling, for instance—because I think we underestimate the potency of the male need to maintain their power.

Piglet in *Winnie the Pooh* referred to sensing something in an "underneath sort of way." That is hard to do.

We can abide scrupulously by the laws, rules, and policies we create in order to assure women an equal opportunity in the corporate workplace and still not overcome the problems that afflicted—and eventually capsized—Raft No. 4.

John and Bill thought that what I wrote was all in my imagination, that it never really happened. "Didn't we try to help them?" they asked. Yes, we did. We told them what to do. We gave them their turns at the helm. We even wrote "left" and "right" on Marlene's hands to help her keep track. But in Piglet's underneath sort of way, we also did everything we could to keep them from succeeding. Why?

Why did our "underneath" behavior conflict so violently with our stated aims? I think it's because we never looked underneath.

When females threaten to move into positions of power, men are threatened twice: first, that they'll lose their authority over the women, and second, that they'll lose prestige and standing with the male, that is, the important, members of the tribe. When I grew up in the Bronx, no self-respecting boy would ever have sponsored a girl into our daily stickball game on the street. Now, as grown businessmen, we still hear that little boy's voice saying, "Hey, get lost. This ain't no girls' game."

We need the laws affirming women's rights. We need the rules and the regulations. But we can't mistake the proclamation of equal opportunity for the realization of it.

I think what we have to do, especially we men, is keep trying to get to our underneath side. Instincts and hormones are mysterious things, not easily understood—and not an excuse for anything. But they are a reason for certain behavior. We need to understand more about what motivates the behavior that lies underneath our surface actions and intentions. Not so that we can justify it, but so that we can change it.

FAITH WOHL *retired at the end of 1993 as a director of human resources at DuPont after a 20-year career at the company. She is now with the U. S. General Services Administration in Washington, D.C., where, as director of workplace initiatives, she oversees child care, elder care, and telecommuting for federal employees.*

The adventure on the Rogue River contains an old and a new lesson. As it describes the behavior of women and men in a work situation, it could have happened yesterday—or perhaps tomorrow—instead of nearly 20 years ago. That constancy is what makes the article a classic.

As a woman who has worked in the business world since the 1950s, I know that what Bob Schrank experienced on the river happens every day in a regular work setting. Sexual tensions and attractions still intrude; men still undermine women unconsciously and deliberately; women still diminish themselves through lack of confidence or experience; and men *and* women are still leery of seeing women in leadership roles. Schrank was right in his revelation—startling as it seemed in the 1970s—that even when you substitute Armanis for Mae Wests, the male-female conflict persists.

Women have fallen short of their goals because we underestimate men's need to maintain their power.

I remember reading the article when it first appeared and seeing it as a mirror that showed clearly what was

happening all around me and my female colleagues. We
all knew with the conviction of our own personal experience and disappointment that it was just these behaviors
that would keep us women from climbing the corporate
ladder. Men would act to preserve their positions of
power, and they knew how to do that with behaviors
both subtle and obvious.

Today I read the story quite differently. Now I see it as
a tale about what happens when managers fail to create
the environment in which a diverse team can achieve
trust and mutual respect. The result was there in a
throwaway line in the story—the raft lost its place in
line. Translation: it lost competitive position. Perhaps in
the smoother waters of the 1970s, when growth and success seemed infinitely possible, the raft could find
another line and try again. Today the discipline of the
marketplace would likely leave the raft on a rock, as it
has left so many well-known enterprises recently.

So Schrank's revealing anecdote is really about what
happens when management fails to address critical
human resource issues in the "permanent white water"
that one leading management consultant has defined as
today's business climate.

Why did this happen on the raft, and what can we
learn from it? It was clear that the men were interested
only in being in charge.
Oddly, they saw that in the
role of helmsman (helmsperson, in clunky 1970s politically correct talk). Yet the
helmsman wasn't really in
charge. In fact, on that raft,
no one was in charge except,
perhaps, the river. As the men struggled to take over
and colluded against the women so they could give

*Today's rapids demand
highly responsive
team members who can
act alone or together
without anyone to lead
them.*

their simplistic orders, they were living out the now-outdated command-and-control style of large bureaucratic organizations. Today's rapids demand something very different—highly responsive work teams whose members can act independently and collectively without being "led" by an order giver.

Read in the context of the 1990s, this classic reveals many points that should concern us. It shows us that diversity cannot be a "flavor-of-the-month" program. Business has talked the language of diversity for the last 20 years without really getting the message. In fact, diversity is a key business strategy that must be learned and practiced because it is linked to the success of the venture. It shows us that creating a team is a complex problem that entails more than simply assigning a group of people to a common task. Creating the environment in which a team can develop from a group of individuals demands thoughtful effort. And the story shows us that success will elude all ventures, whether boating or business, led by people who do not understand these lessons, especially when the current is as swift and the water is as roiled as it is in the business world today.

SHEILA WELLINGTON *is president of Catalyst, the independent not-for-profit organization that works with business and the professions to effect change for women through research, advisory services, and communication.*

While the Bill, Bob, and John of 1994 might still behave as corrosively as they did in 1977, a trip down the Rogue River today would reveal a much changed Marlene and Helen. They wouldn't for a minute sit back passively and let the men take over the helm because they are "so much better" at steering. In the last 17 years, women have learned a few things. One of them is that leading a business today has very little to do with white-water rafting and shooting the rapids.

The metaphor of Raft No. 4 is dated. The world of enterprise no longer revolves around the physical strength of the male hunter who slays the beast and drags it home (or the prowess of the river navigator, for that matter). Today's successful business "warrior" is marked by an awareness of the changing world and the leadership and team-building skills that bespeak brains, not brawn, metaphorical or otherwise.

The Marlenes and Helens of today are just as educated as the Bills and Bobs, if not more so. In 1991, women earned more bachelor's degrees (53.9%) and master's degrees (53.5%) than men (compared with 46.1% and 47% respectively in 1977). They also earned 43% of all law degrees (up from 22.4% in 1977) and more than one-third of all MBAs (compared with just one out of seven in 1977).

Furthermore, women have entered the ranks of corporate management. The percentage of executive, administrative, and managerial employees who are female has exploded from a mere 2.5% in 1977 to 42% in 1993. Although women have not attained the highest reaches of corporate management in large numbers, there is a critical mass in the pipeline. In 1977, 46 women were directors of America's leading corporations. Today there are 500 such women—not nearly enough, to be sure, but more than ten times as many as 15 years ago.

I won't rule out the possibility that one or more of the men on the raft might have changed, too, in 17 years. Many progressive companies today are led by men who have responded positively to the challenge of assimilating women into their workplaces. They're smart enough to seek the best talent in whatever shape, size, and color it comes. They know that if Marlene and Helen don't get their turn at the helm and the support they need to do the job, there's a good chance that at least one of them will leave to paddle her own canoe. (By the way, fellas, it just might turn out to be an ocean liner.) Such leaders have come to realize that we're all in the same raft and that whether or not we stay dry depends less on the brawn of the helmsperson than on the collective skill of the team and its members.

ELEANOR PETERSEN *was the first woman chair of the Illinois Fair Employment Practices Commission, a founder and officer of a federal savings and loan created to make mortgage loans to minorities, and founder and president of the Donors Forum of Chicago, a regional association of grant makers. She has been retired for eight years and lives in Chicago.*

I was "Helen" in Bob Schrank's raft, and when I read his article in this magazine 17 years ago, it made me angry. I was angry at Bob and the other two men for the games they'd played, and I was very angry—and chagrined—at my own failure to realize what was going on. It took the article to show me just how loaded the deck had been against us.

Now, 17 years later, I'm still angry. Not at Bob, whose insight into his own behavior was illuminating and, in fact, courageous, and no longer at myself, because I have worked hard to make things better for women and minorities. I am angry at U.S. society. I am impatient and discouraged at how little progress we have made in almost 20 years. I have come to believe that the power structures of our political, educational, and corporate institutions are deeply conservative and authoritarian,

that the authorities they conserve are still overwhelm-
ingly male and white, and that change is insultingly slow.

It takes time, we're told, to rise through the pipeline
in any profession or organization. How much time?
Women have been pushing hard against the glass ceiling
on business promotions for at least 30 years, but 30 years
is not enough. Blacks have been pressing for equal
opportunity since the end of the Civil War, but five gen-
erations is not enough. The suffragist movement began
its struggle for equal political rights more than a century
ago, and we now have 7 women senators out of 100. Are
we supposed to be proud of that achievement? Wouldn't
shame be a more appropriate reaction? The pipeline
argument is a sham and a disgrace.

For many years, I've worked with foundations. Over
the last two decades, in order to get more money for
women, we've made a huge, successful effort to get foundations to hire more women and an equal, much *less*
successful effort to move
them up to decision-
making jobs and to seats
on foundation boards. In
that whole 20 years,
foundation grants to
women's and girls' organizations have risen from 3% of
total foundation giving—to 4%. So now, at last, women
have begun to set up their own foundations, run by
women to raise money for women.

Today I'd **make** *the men give
me responsibility. You
can't be polite about change.
You have to be rude.*

Women, especially young women, have to start doing
the same kind of thing in business and politics, because
the pace of "acceptable" change is too courteous, too
ladylike, too accommodating. Many in my generation
went along with that leisurely, unproductive rate of
change, exactly the way Marlene and I went along in that

raft. We let the men take care of us. We allowed ourselves to be comfortable and irresponsible. We were all
victims, of course, men and women alike, because
instead of learning new skills and new ways to work
together, we all just repeated old roles in an old, authoritarian world.

Today I would no longer let that happen. I would
make myself take the helm and the responsibility no
matter how frightened I was. And I would make the men
give it to me. You can't bring about change politely. You
have to be tough. You have to be rude.

Before the civil rights movement, people said to
blacks, "Don't try to move too fast." But after 100 years of
waiting, they lost patience and so took change into their
own hands. Women must do the same.

Originally published in May–June 1994
Reprint 94308

Winning the Talent War for Women

Sometimes It Takes a Revolution

DOUGLAS M. MCCRACKEN

Executive Summary

IN 1991 DELOITTE & TOUCHE got a wake-up call about its efforts to retain women professionals. While it was recruiting almost as many women as men, the company had a much higher turnover rate for women.

Many in the firm thought Deloitte was doing everything it could to retain talented women, but when they looked harder, they found otherwise. Most women weren't leaving to raise families; they were leaving after having weighed their unpromising career options in Deloitte's male-dominated culture. CEO Mike Cook led the way in making a business case—not a moral or emotional one—for change. Next, the company held mandatory, two-day, intensive workshops for its 5,000 U.S. managers. Case vignettes and discussions brought out subtle gender-based assumptions about careers and aspirations that had discouraged high-performing women from staying.

The workshops were instrumental in convincing a critical mass of partners to join the effort, and the firm began to monitor the progress of women to ensure they received their share of mentoring and premier assignments. Executive compensation became linked to how successfully units implemented a flexible menu of goals. And other policies promoted a better balance between work and life for both men and women. Finally, an external advisory council kept the firm's feet to the fire.

Deloitte's gender gap in turnover has now nearly vanished, and the number of women partners and directors is the highest among the Big Five. These cultural changes weren't easy, but they've enabled Deloitte to grow faster than any of its competitors.

NINE YEARS AGO, we came to grips with the fact that women at Deloitte were on the march—out the door. In 1991, only four of our 50 candidates for partner were women, even though Deloitte & Touche—America's third largest accounting, tax, and consulting firm at the time—had been heavily recruiting women from colleges and business schools since 1980. Not only that. We also found that women were leaving the firm at a significantly greater rate than men.

To be frank, many of the firm's senior partners, including myself, didn't actually see the exodus of women as a problem, or at least, it wasn't *our* problem. We assumed that women were leaving to have children and stay home. If there was a problem at all, it was society's or the women's, not Deloitte's. In fact, most senior partners firmly believed we were doing everything possible to retain women. We prided ourselves on our open, collegial, performance-based work environment.

How wrong we were, and how far we've come.

Over the next few years, we analyzed why women were leaving and worked to stop the outflow. At first, the program was largely our CEO's idea; unlike many of us, he saw women's leaving as a serious business matter that the firm could and should fix.

These days, you'd be hard-pressed to find partners within the firm who disagree. It took a cultural revolution, but Deloitte now has a radically different approach to retaining talented women. Based on six principles, it is an approach that other companies might well consider, for its results speak for themselves.

Today 14% of our partners and directors are women. While we aren't yet where we want to be, this percentage is up from 5% in 1991 and the highest in the Big Five. The number of women managing partners has increased dramatically, and we've eliminated the gender gap in our turnover: women now stay on at about the

In professional services firms, the "product" is talent, billed to the client by the hour; and so much of our firm's product was leaving at an alarming rate.

same rate as men each year. The firm's annual turnover rate as a whole fell from around 25% in the early 1990s to 18% in 1999, despite an intensifying war for talent. Besides saving us $250 million in hiring and training costs, lower turnover has enabled Deloitte to grow faster than any other large professional services firm in the past several years.

A Two-Stage Process

Deloitte's Initiative for the Retention and Advancement of Women grew out of a 1992 task force chaired by

Mike Cook, then CEO of Deloitte & Touche. A number of women partners initially wanted nothing to do with the effort because it implied affirmative action. But Cook, along with a handful of partners—women and men—insisted that high turnover for women was a problem of the utmost urgency. In professional services firms, they argued, the "product" is talent, billed to the client by the hour; and so much of our firm's product was leaving at an alarming rate. Cook made sure that both women and men were part of the task force and that it represented a broad range of views, including outright skepticism.

Once in place, the task force didn't immediately launch a slew of new organizational policies aimed at outlawing bad behavior. Instead, it approached the problem methodically, just as we would approach a consulting assignment. Thus, it first investigated the problem and gathered the data necessary to make a business case—not a moral or emotional one—for change. Then it prepared the groundwork for change by holding a series of intensive, two-day workshops for all of our management professionals. These sessions were designed to bring to the surface the gender-based assumptions about careers and aspirations that had discouraged high-performing women from staying.

Only then did the firm announce a series of policies aimed at keeping women. A major component of these policies was to first get all the firm's offices to monitor the progress of their women professionals. The head of every office received the message that the CEO and other managing partners were watching, and in turn, women started getting their share of premier client assignments and informal mentoring. Other policies, designed to promote more balance between work and life for women and men, also helped. These efforts have opened up our work environment and our culture in ways we never expected.

Preparing the Way for Change

Along the way, we've learned a series of lessons. Other companies, with different traditions and operating environments, may well follow other paths to achieve equitable treatment of men and women. But we think our lessons will apply to a great many organizations.

Make sure senior management is front and center. Despite its name, the Women's Initiative was always driven by the managing partners—it never became an "HR thing" foisted on the firm. Like other organizations, we were used to having new personnel programs every so often, just one more thing added to an already full plate. I'm sure most of our partners felt initially that the focus on women was the latest "program of the year"; we would try our best and then move on to something else. But from the start, senior management signaled that the initiative would be led by the partners. Cook named Ellen Gabriel, a star partner, as the first leader of the initiative.

Most women weren't leaving to raise families; they had weighed their options in Deloitte's male-dominated culture and found them wanting.

Cook's own leadership involved no small investment and risk. In a firm like ours, where the partners are also owners, leadership is not top-down. He took charge of the effort personally and visibly, and with every step, we all got the sense that change was a high priority for him.

In Cook's case, a reputation for toughness helped to give this initiative credibility.

Make an airtight business case for cultural change. The task force prepared the firm for change by laying a foundation of data, including personal stories. Deloitte was doing a great job of hiring high-performing women; in fact, women often earned higher performance ratings than men in their first years with the firm. Yet the percentage of women decreased with each step up the career ladder, in all practices and regions, and many women left the firm just when they were expected to receive promotions. Interviews with current and former women professionals explained why. Most weren't leaving to raise families; they had weighed their options in Deloitte's male-dominated culture and found them wanting. Many of them, dissatisfied with a culture they perceived as endemic to professional services firms, switched professions. And all of them together represented a major lost opportunity for the firm.

These facts made for a sobering report to the senior partners on the firm's management committee in 1993. As Cook summarized, "Half of our hires are now women, and almost all of them have left before becoming partner candidates. We know that in order to get enough partners to grow the business, we're going to have to go deeper and deeper into the pool of new hires. Are you willing to have more and more of your partners taken from lower and lower in the talent pool? *And* let the high-performing women go elsewhere in the marketplace?"

Let the world watch you. With the endorsement of the management committee, the firm moved forward. It held a press conference to launch the Women's Initiative, but it also went further and named an external advisory council. Chaired by Lynn Martin, former U.S. secretary of labor, the council comprised business leaders with expertise in the area of women in the workplace. Besides reviewing the initiative's progress, the council brought visibility to the effort. As the task force realized, going public would put healthy pressure on the partners to commit to change and deliver results. And that's what happened, particularly with slow-moving offices in the organization. Local managers received prodding comments from their associates like, "I read in the *Wall Street Journal* that we're doing this major initiative, but I don't see big change in our office."

The council has held the firm's feet to the fire in a variety of ways: an annual report on the initiative; periodic voice mail updates from Lynn Martin to the entire firm; and full-day meetings of the council with the firm's senior executives. The council defines the challenges we still face, and it lets senior management know they're not off the hook.

Along with helping the task force think about gender, the council has opened the firm's eyes to broader issues. In 1994, the council was meeting with a group of eight professionals—four men and four women—identified by their managers as rising stars at Deloitte. At the end of the meeting, one member of the council asked, almost as an afterthought, "How many of you want to be partners next time we see you?" Only one of the eight said yes. Stunned, the council asked for an explanation.

They were surprised to find that young men in the firm didn't want what older men wanted; they weren't trying to buy good enough lifestyles so that their wives didn't have to work. At the time, the average partner at Deloitte was making $350,000 and working 80 hours a

week, but these young people—men and women both—
would've been happy working 60 hours a week for
$250,000. They believed they were good enough, and they
weren't willing to give up their families and outside lives
for another $100,000. One council member recalls,
"When we asked if they wanted to be partners, we
thought they were going to salute and thank us and hope
we put nice letters in their files. Instead they looked at us
and said, 'Perhaps.'"

Begin with dialogue as the platform for change.
The task force had found that women at Deloitte perceived they had fewer career opportunities than men,
but no one could point to any specific policies as the cul-
prits. We had to tackle our underlying culture to fix the
problem. Accordingly, the firm held special two-day
workshops designed to explore issues of gender in the
workplace. We needed to begin a dialogue: in our view,
the key to creating cultural change in the firm was to
turn taboo subjects at work into acceptable topics of
discussion.

During 1992 and 1993, nearly every management professional at Deloitte & Touche—5,000 people, including
the board of directors, the management committee, and
the managing partners of all of our U.S. offices—
attended the workshop in groups of 24. Cook personally
monitored attendance; as one partner puts it, "Resistance was futile." Many harbored doubts. I myself saw it
as just one more thing to do, and I had always been skeptical of HR-type programs. I'm sure I wasn't the only
partner calculating in my head the lost revenue represented by two days' worth of billable hours, multiplied by
5,000—not to mention the $8 million cost of the work-
shops themselves.

I was dead wrong. The workshops were a turning point, a pivotal event in the life of the firm. Through discussions, videos, and case studies, we began to take a hard look at how gender

Women get evaluated on their performance; men get evaluated on their potential.

attitudes affected the environment at Deloitte. It wasn't enough to hear the problems in the abstract; we had to see them face to face. Sitting across a table from a respected colleague and hearing her say, "Why did you make that assumption about women? It's just not true," I, like many others, began to change.

The lightbulbs went on for different partners at different times. Many of us had little exposure to dual-career families but did have highly educated daughters entering the workforce. A woman partner would say to a male counterpart, "Sarah's graduating from college. Would you want her to work for a company that has lower expectations for women?" Suddenly he'd get it.

Case studies were useful for bringing out and examining subtle differences in expectations. Drawing on scripts provided by outside facilitators, people in the workshops would break into groups, discuss cases, and share solutions with the full group. A typical scenario would have partners evaluating two promising young professionals, a woman and a man with identical skills. Of the woman, a partner would say, "She's really good, she gives 100%. But I just don't see her interacting with a CFO. She's not as polished as some. Her presentation skills could be stronger." The conversation about the man would vary slightly, but significantly: "He's good. He and I are going to take a CFO golfing next week. I know he can grow into it; he has tremendous potential."

Beginning with these subtle variations in language,
careers could go in very different directions. A woman
was found a bit wanting, and we (male partners) couldn't
see how she would get to the next level. As one woman
summed up, "Women get evaluated on their performance; men get evaluated on their potential."

Another scenario had two members of a team arriving
late for an early-morning meeting. Both were single parents, one a father and one a mother. The team joked
about and then forgot the man's tardiness but assumed
the woman was having child-care problems. After the
meeting, the team leader, a woman, suggested that she
think seriously about her priorities.

Senarios like these lent realism to the workshop discussions, and hard-hitting dialogue often ensued. One
partner was jolted into thinking about an outing he was
going to attend, an annual "guys' weekend" with partners
from the Atlanta office and many of their clients. It was
very popular, and there were never any women. It hadn't
occurred to him to ask why. He figured "no woman
would want to go to a golf outing where you smoke
cigars and drink beer and tell lies." But the women in the
session were quick to say that by not being there, they
were frozen out of informal networks where important
information was shared and a sense of belonging built.
Today women are routinely included in such outings.

Work assignments got a lot of attention in the workshops. Everyone knew that high-profile, high-revenue
assignments were the key to advancement in the firm.
Careers were made on big clients; you grew up on the
Microsoft engagement, the Chrysler engagement. But the
process of assigning these plum accounts was largely
unexamined. Too often, women were passed over for
certain assignments because male partners made
assumptions about what they wanted: "I wouldn't put

her on that kind of company because it's a tough manufacturing environment," or "That client is difficult to deal
with." Even more common, "Travel puts too much pressure on women," or "Her husband won't go along with
relocating." Usually we weren't even conscious of making
such assumptions, but the workshops brought them
front and center.

The workshops also highlighted one of the worst
aspects of these hidden assumptions: they were self-
fulfilling. Say a partner gets a big new client and asks the
assignment director to put together a team, adding,
"Continuity is very important on this engagement." The
assignment director knows that women turn over more
rapidly than men and has the numbers to prove it. So
the thinking goes, "If I put a woman on this account, the
partner will be all over me—and that's who evaluates
me." In the end, John gets to work on the big account
and Jane works "somewhere else." After a while, Jane
says, "I'm not going anywhere here. I'm never going to
get the big opportunities," so she leaves. And the assignment director says, "I knew it."

The task force realized the workshops were risky; the
firm was opening a can of worms and couldn't control
the results. Indeed, a few of the workshops flopped, dis-
integrating into a painful mixture of bitterness and skepticism. Some people dismissed the experience as a waste
of time. But ultimately the workshops converted a critical mass of Deloitte's leaders. The message was out: don't
make assumptions about what women do or don't want.
Ask them.

Putting the New Attitudes to Work

The workshops generated momentum, but the dialogue
had to be followed with concrete operational steps if we

were going to bring about real change. The task force
had clear expectations: more of our qualified women
should be promoted, and the turnover rate for women
should fall. But the firm had to be careful not to set
quotas or seem to give women all the plum assignments. The key was to send a clear, powerful message
for change while still giving heads of local offices some
discretion.

Use a flexible system of accountability. Since the
fastest way to change behaviors is to measure them,
the task force started by simply asking for numbers.
Beginning in 1993, in the midst of the workshops, local
offices were asked to conduct annual reviews to determine if the top-rated women were receiving their pro-
portionate share of the best assignments. Some offices
resisted, questioning the usefulness of this time-
consuming exercise or fearing that the initiative would
lead to quotas. However, a few pointed phone calls
from the CEO prodded the laggards. The reviews con-
firmed our suspicions: women tended to be assigned to
projects in nonprofit, health care, and retail—segments
that generally lacked large global accounts—while men
received most of the assignments in manufacturing,
financial services, and highly visible areas like mergers
and acquisitions.

The reviews had their intended effect. Like many
other managing partners, I began routinely discussing
assignment decisions with the partners in charge of project staffing to make sure women had opportunities for
key engagements. Most offices began tracking the activities of their high-performing women on a quarterly basis.
To complement the connections that men naturally
made with one another, we began hosting regular net-

working events for women—for example, panel discussions where women partners discussed their careers and leadership roles, followed by networking receptions. We also started formal career planning for women partners and senior managers. This planning proved so helpful that women suggested men also be included, thus giving rise to Deloitte Consulting's current Partner Development Program.

Only after the operational changes had percolated through the organization did the task force introduce clear accountability for the changes that were being made. It offered offices a menu of goals derived from the Women's Initiative—such as a recruiting hit rate or a reduction in the gender gap in turnover—yet left it up to the offices to pick the goals best suited for their particular situations. Office heads started including their choices among the objectives that drove their year-end evaluations and compensation. And the firm made sure that results on turnover, promotion, and other key numbers for each office were circulated widely among management, feeding a healthy internal competitiveness. Low-performing offices got calls or visits from task force members to push for better progress. Today partners know that they will not become leaders of this organization if they have not demonstrated their commitment to the Women's Initiative.

It's Not Just About Women

Moving toward equality in career development was fundamental. But as people began to discuss gender issues in workshops, meetings, and hallways, what started out as a program for women soon began to affect our overall corporate culture.

Promote work-life balance for men and women.
We discovered that work-life balance was important to
everyone. On paper, we had always allowed temporary,
flexible work arrangements, but people believed (rightly,
at the time) that working fewer hours could doom an
otherwise promising career. In 1993, only a few hundred
people were taking advantage of the policy. So now we
said that opting for flexible work wouldn't hinder
advancement in the firm, though it might stretch out the
time required for promotion. Use of these arrangements
became one more benchmark of an office's progress with
the initiative. And when a woman was admitted to the
partnership in 1995 while on a flexible work arrangement, people really began to get the message. By 1999
more than 30 people on flexible work arrangements had
made partner, and in that year, the total number of people on flexible schedules had doubled to 800.

We also reexamined the schedule that all of us work,
especially within the consulting practice. A grinding
travel schedule had long been an accepted part of the
macho consultants' culture. Typically, a consultant was
away from home five days a week, for up to 18 months at
a time. In 1996, we started a new schedule, dubbed the
3-4-5 program. Consultants working on out-of-town
projects were to be away from home three nights a week,
at the client site four days a week, and in their local
Deloitte offices on the fifth day.

The 3-4-5 schedule hasn't been feasible on all projects—for example, those with tight deadlines like Y2K-
driven system implementations. In fact, many of us were
concerned initially that the program would compromise
client service. But most clients embraced our new program. It turned out that employees from the client's
regional offices were exhausted, too, by traveling to meet

Deloitte's team at their home offices all week long. One day each week without the Deloitte consultants at their sites was a relief, not an inconvenience! By breaking the collective silence about the personal price everyone was paying, we made everyone happier. We now expect the vast majority of all projects to conform to 3-4-5.

As a result of these and other changes, we've transformed our culture into one in which people are comfortable talking about aspects of their personal lives, going well beyond client assignments and career development. Teams are getting requests like "I want to talk to my kids every night at 7:00 for half an hour," or "I'd really like to go to the gym in the morning, so can we start our meetings at 8:30 instead of 7:30?" This more open environment not only helps us keep our rising stars but also makes us more creative in a variety of areas.

A New Outlook

The changes at Deloitte are by no means complete. For many years, women have made up one-third to one-half of Deloitte's recruits, so we need to make sure the percentage of women partners and directors rises well above 14%. And we face new challenges. Now that more women are becoming partners, how can we make sure they continue to develop and advance into positions of leadership? In an increasingly global firm, how can we extend the values of the initiative while respecting local cultural differences?

Still, we have transformed our work environment, even in the smallest details. When a visiting speaker— even a client—cracks a joke at women's expense, none of us laughs, not even politely. One partner turned down an invitation to join a premier lunch club in Manhattan when he learned it excluded women. And we've opened our eyes to differences in style that go beyond gender to include culture. For example, on a recent client engagement, the project manager described an Asian consultant on his team as "shy" and therefore not ready to take on more responsibility. But another partner pushed the project manager for details and suggested that consultants could still be successful even if they didn't "command a room" or raise their voices when speaking in meetings.

We've not only narrowed the gender gap; we've narrowed the gap between who we think we are and who we truly are. Now when I say ours is a meritocracy, I'm speaking about men and women. It's not easy to manage a diverse group of people; we have to be creative and flexible in developing coaching and mentoring capabilities. Although the Women's Initiative has made managing more complicated, the benefits are substantial: greater creativity, faster growth, and far greater performance for our clients.

Lessons from Deloitte's Women's Initiative

Make sure senior management is front and center.
To overcome the resistance of partners, the CEO actively led the Women's Initiative. He put his own reputation on the line.

Make an airtight business case for cultural change.
Emotional appeals weren't going to be enough. We had to document the business imperative for change before we could justify the investment and effort that the initiative would require.

Let the world watch you. We appointed an external advisory council and told the press about our plans. They wouldn't let the initiative be another "program of the year" that led nowhere.

Begin with dialogue as the platform for change. We required everyone to attend intensive workshops to reveal and examine gender-based assumptions in mentoring and client assignments.

Use a flexible system of accountability. We first required local offices to measure their efforts with women professionals. Next, we worked with the office heads to select their focus areas for change under the initiative.

Promote work-life balance for men and women. Policies for flexible work arrangements and lighter travel schedules not only eased the strain on busy professionals but also helped open our corporate culture.

Originally published in November–December 2000
Reprint R00611

Is This the Right Time to Come Out?

ALISTAIR D. WILLIAMSON

Executive Summary

IN THIS FICTIONAL CASE STUDY, Adam Lawson is a promising young associate at Kirkham McDowell Securities, a St. Louis underwriting and financial advisory firm. Recently, Adam helped to bring in an extremely lucrative deal, and soon he and a few other associates will be honored for their efforts at the firm's silver anniversary dinner.

George Campbell, vice president in mergers and acquisitions, is caught unprepared when Adam tells him that, after serious reflection, he has decided to bring his partner, Robert Collins, to the banquet. George is one of Adam's biggest supporters at the firm, and he personally has no problem with Adam being gay.

But it is one thing for Adam to come out of the closet at the office. It is quite another to do so at a public company-client event. After all, Kirkham McDowell's client roster

includes some very conservative companies—one of the
country's largest defense contractors, for example.
George is concerned with how Adam's openness about
his sexual orientation will play with their clients and, as a
result, how senior management will react.

Adam has *not* come to George for permission to
bring Robert to the dinner. But clearly Adam wants some
sort of response. George has never faced sexual diversity issues in the workplace before, and there is no company policy to guide him. Just how negative an effect
could Robert have on Adam's career with the firm and
the firm's relationship with its clients? Isn't it possible that
even the firm's most conservative clients will simply
decide that Adam's choice of guest is a personal matter—not a business one?

Seven experts comment on George's dilemma and
discuss issues of sexual diversity in the workplace.

GEORGE CAMPBELL, assistant vice president in
mergers and acquisitions at Kirkham McDowell Securities, a St. Louis underwriting and financial advisory firm,
looked up as Adam Lawson, one of his most promising
associates, entered his office. Adam, 29 years old, had
been with the firm for only two years but had already
distinguished himself as having great potential. Recently,
he had helped to bring in an extremely lucrative deal,
and in six weeks, he and several other associates would
be honored for their efforts at the firm's silver anniversary dinner.

As Adam closed the door and sat down, he said,
"George, I'd like to talk to you about the banquet. I've

thought about this very carefully, and I want you to know that I plan to bring my partner, Robert Collins, as my escort."

George was taken aback. "Well, Adam," he said, "I don't quite know what to say. I have to be honest with you; I'm a little surprised. I had no idea that you were gay. I would never have guessed." He looked at Adam for clues on how to proceed: his subordinate did seem nervous but not defiant or hostile.

Though only a 50-person operation, Kirkham McDowell had long since secured its status as one of the region's leading corporate financial advisers. The firm's client roster included established and successful regional companies as well as one of the country's largest defense contractors, a very conservative company for which the firm managed part of an impressive pension portfolio. Representatives of Kirkham McDowell's major clients and many of the area's most influential political and business leaders were expected to attend the banquet. All this raced through George's mind as he asked Adam, "Why do you want to do this? Why do you want to mix your personal and professional lives?"

"For the same reason that you bring your wife to company social events," Adam replied.

A look of confusion flickered across George's face while Adam continued. "Think about it for a moment, George. Success in this business depends in great part on the relationships you develop with your clients and the people you work with. An important part of those relationships is letting people know about your life away from the office, and that includes the people who are important to you. Some of the other associates already know Robert. Whenever his schedule permits,

he accompanies me when I'm invited by one of my colleagues to have dinner with his or her spouse. Granted,
that isn't very often—Robert is a corporate attorney,
and his work is very demanding—but he joins me
whenever he can."

"But, Adam, a wife isn't the same thing as a—"

"It *is* the same thing, George. Robert and I have made
a commitment to each other. We have been together for
almost five years now, and I would feel very uncomfortable telling him that I was going to a major social event
alone—on a weekend, no less."

"Well, I'm sure you'd agree that it wouldn't be appropriate for an associate to bring a date—someone he
barely knows—to such an event."

"Come on, George. I think you know me well enough
to realize that I have better judgment than that. If Robert
and I had known each other for only six months, I
wouldn't be having this conversation with you right now.
But, as I said, we've been together for over five years!"

George thought for a moment. "Adam," he said slowly,
"I'm just not sure you should try to make an issue of this
at such an important time for the company. Why bring it
up now? Think of our clients. We work with some very
conservative companies. They could very well decide to
give their business to a firm whose views seem to agree
more with their own. You're not just making a personal
statement here. You're saying something about the culture at Kirkham McDowell, something that some of our
clients might fundamentally oppose. How are they going
to react?"

Adam leaned forward. "This is only an issue if people
make it an issue," he said. "I have resolved never to lie
about myself or about anything that is important to
me—and that includes my sexuality. Since I joined the

firm, as I've become comfortable sharing details of my personal life with certain colleagues, I've come out to them and often introduced them to Robert. If people ask me if I'm gay, I'm honest with them. Likewise, if people ask me if I have a girlfriend, I tell them about my relationship with Robert. With the silver anniversary celebration coming up, I thought the time was right to speak with you. This is the first large social event the company has held since I started working here. And after a lot of discussion with Robert and some of the associates here, I've decided that I need to be as open at the banquet as I have tried to be in other areas within the organization.

"It's not a decision that I've taken lightly. I've seen what has happened to some of my gay friends who have come out at work. Even at much less conservative companies, some are never invited to important social events with colleagues and customers, no matter how much business they bring in. They'll never know whether or not their bonuses have been affected by prejudice related to their sexuality. I know my career could be adversely influenced by this decision, but I believe that my work should stand on its own merits. George, I've been a top contributor at this firm since I walked in the door. I hope I can rely on you to back me up in this."

Adam stood up but waited for George to reply. "You've given me a lot to think about," George said. "And I don't want to say anything until I've had a chance to consider all the implications. I appreciate the confidence you've shown in me by being so open. I wish I had something conclusive to say at this point, but the fact of the matter is that I have never had to face this issue before. I am one of your biggest supporters here at the firm. Your work has been exemplary. And, until today, I would have said that you could look forward to a very successful career here. But I'm concerned about how this will play with our clients and, as a result, about how senior management will react. I personally don't have any problems with your being gay, but I'd hate to see you torpedo your career over this. It's possible that this could jeopardize some of our relationships with significant clients. Let me think about it for a few days. We can have lunch next week and map out a strategy."

After Adam left his office, George sat in silence for a few minutes, trying to make sense of the conversation. He was unsure of his next move. Adam clearly had *not* come into his office looking for permission to bring his lover to the banquet. George realized that he could do nothing and let events simply unfold. After all, Adam had not asked that Robert be included in his benefits coverage nor had he requested a specific managerial decision. There was no company policy on paper to guide him through his dilemma. But Adam wouldn't have come to him if he hadn't wanted a response of some kind. And shouldn't he at least tell his superior in order to head off any awkward moments at the banquet?

Just how negative an effect could Robert have on Adam's career with the firm and on the firm's relationship with its clients? Wasn't it possible, even likely, that the party would come off without incident? That the issue would blow over? That even the firm's most conservative clients wouldn't realize the significance of Adam's guest or would simply decide that it was a personal issue, not a business one? Or would George's worst fears be realized? Adam had to recognize that the potential risks were great. It was one thing for him to come out of the closet at the office. But wasn't he pushing things too far?

How Should George Respond to Adam's Disclosure?

Seven experts examine issues of discrimination in the workplace.

JAMES D. WOODS *is assistant professor of communications at the College of Staten Island/CUNY. He is the coauthor of* The Corporate Closet: The Professional Lives of Gay Men in America *with Jay H. Lucas.*

As lesbian and gay workers become an increasingly visible part of the work force, sooner or later every manager will stand in George Campbell's shoes. Some of them, like George, will be asked for their advice or blessing as a subordinate plans his or her exit from the closet. Others will encounter the issue more obliquely. They will participate in a promo-

The firm owes Adam the same opportunities given to his heterosexual peers.

tion, compensation, or hiring decision involving a lesbian or gay worker. They will have to revisit a nondiscrimination policy that ignores sexual orientation or reevaluate a benefits program that excludes same-sex couples. They will be sought as mentors, tennis partners, and lunch companions by coworkers who they know or suspect to be gay. Like George, they may find themselves on unfamiliar turf.

Above all, managers should guide their responses by a commitment to fairness. To his credit, George has already focused on the central facts of Adam's situation. Kirkham McDowell has invited employees to bring their spouses to its silver anniversary dinner. Adam wants to bring his partner, Robert, a man with whom he shares a serious and committed relationship. Ethically speaking, the solution is obvious: Kirkham McDowell must encourage Adam to bring Robert, extending to him the same invitation given to other guests. Anything less amounts to discrimination, plain and simple.

Some will say, of course, that it is inappropriate for Adam to be so public about his sexuality, that he should strive to keep personal and professional matters apart. Yet this objection, however familiar, is based on a blatant double standard. If the firm is to be fair, it owes Adam the same opportunities given to his heterosexual peers, including the right to be frank about his sexuality. In most work settings, heterosexuality is continuously on display, ubiquitous to the point that we often fail to notice it. It is alluded to in benefits policies, in dress and self-presentation, in jokes and gossip, in symbols like wedding rings and baby pictures. Coworkers discuss their families, friends, and loved ones, and the sharing of sexual information often grounds such intangibles as rapport, loyalty, and trust.

Indeed, much "work" is in fact the management of relationships, which means that men and women's personal qualifications are inevitably part of the job. When judging the professional competence of our peers, for example, we routinely take so-called personal traits into consideration. We ponder how well a particular coworker fits in with the group, what kind of chemistry he or she has with customers, or how well he or she sees eye-to-eye with a particular client, all without realizing that there is a sexual dimension to these questions. As Adam points out, business is based on relationships, and relationships wither when one is evasive about personal, family, or romantic matters. Given the countless ways in which personal and professional lives overlap, it is disingenuous to argue that it is Adam who is confusing the two by bringing his partner to a company dinner.

However, there is a second consideration that involves not ethics but the bottom line. One can hardly fault George for worrying about how Adam's gesture will be received by clients. When he frets about the potential cost to the firm, he is simply being a responsible manager. What George should reconsider, however, is his definition of these costs. Rather than ask if Kirkham McDowell can afford to be fair, George should consider what the alternative would cost his firm.

First, George should realize that his decision will send a message to a potentially large number of men and women. As a percentage of the labor pool, lesbian and gay workers probably outnumber Hispanics, Asian-Pacific Islanders, the disabled, and others whom we have traditionally classified as minorities. (If we accept the standard estimate that 10% of the population is lesbian or gay, they also outnumber African-Americans, who represent 12.5% of the population but only 5.6% of the professional work force.)

That message, therefore, could have serious consequences for the performance of a large number of employees. Over the past three years, my own study of gay professionals identified several negative consequences of discrimination on the basis of sexual orientation. Most obviously, lesbian and gay workers are less productive when they are consumed by the fear of exposure. To protect themselves, some invent elaborate schemes to disguise their sexuality, deceptions that waste precious time. Others try to avoid the subject of sexuality altogether by withdrawing from the social life of the office but find that this too has its costs. They pay for their privacy with limited interpersonal effectiveness, reduced job satisfaction, and feelings of isolation. Even those who come out, as Adam did, sacrifice time and energy to the task. How many hours did Adam spend worrying about whom to tell, how they would respond, and what it would mean for his career? As Adam points out, "It's not a decision I've taken lightly." Kirkham McDowell has gained nothing by making the decision difficult.

Over time, some of these men and women will simply abandon their employers, taking with them whatever investment has been made in their development. Some will migrate toward more hospitable employers, ensuring a talent drain at those companies that make them feel unwelcome. Others will abandon large organizations altogether, some to accept "safe" jobs beneath their abilities, some to start their own businesses. My own survey found, for example, that half of all lesbian and gay professionals took sexual orientation issues into consideration when selecting their current place of employment. Many had left or turned down jobs with companies that they considered to be homophobic. In Adam's case, there can be little doubt that these issues are a key consideration. If his request to bring Robert is rebuffed, the firm should expect, sooner or later, to lose him.

Finally, George should not be too quick to assume the worst of his clients. Some may be offended by the sight of a male couple, just as some are offended by other ethnic, religious, or political groups in our increasingly diverse labor pool. Yet lesbians and gay men who come out in the workplace very often find the opposite to be the case. For many, their disclosure precipitates a flood of support. New opportunities emerge. Alliances materialize in unexpected places. Key relationships deepen. Clients and coworkers applaud them for their courage.

It is possible, of course, that Kirkham McDowell will lose a client or two. But, on balance, discrimination is never good for business. Some of George's clients are undoubtedly gay. Many of them have friends, children, or parents who are lesbian or gay, as do many of his potential clients. A growing number of companies—including AT&T, Levi Strauss & Co., 3M, and Digital—currently have nondiscrimination policies that include sexual orientation and select their business partners accordingly. By choosing the ethical solution, Kirkham McDowell stands to gain at least as much as it risks to lose.

George is absolutely right when he says that Adam would be "saying something about the culture at Kirkham McDowell" by bringing his partner to a company function. By welcoming Robert into its extended family, the firm would be saying that it respects the dignity of its employees, that it values the diversity of its work force. It would send a clear message, to clients as well as employees, that bigotry has no place within its walls. What will Kirkham McDowell be saying, both to Adam and to its clients, if it doesn't?

JOHN M. CONLEY *holds the Ivey Research Chair at the University of North Carolina Law School. He is also adjunct professor of cultural anthropology at Duke University.*

WILLIAM M. O'BARR *is professor and chair of cultural anthropology at Duke University and adjunct professor of law and anthropology at the University of North Carolina at Chapel Hill. Their principal research interests involve the use of anthropological methods to study U.S. institutions.*

We are struck initially by the fact that Adam and
George agree on one fundamental point: the importance
of non-financial factors to their firm's success in the
financial world. Adam argues that the firm's business
depends on personal relationships with clients and that
disclosure of one's personal life helps foster such relationships. George counters that Adam's proposed disclosure would make a statement about Kirkham McDowell's culture that might be false, displeasing to clients, or
both. Will pension fund managers and other clients actually base their evaluation of Kirkham McDowell on anything but the firm's investment performance?

The answer is an emphatic yes. An anthropological
study of large pension funds that we recently completed
shows compellingly that as long as money management
firms perform within a broad band of respectability, pension executives judge them on the basis of ad hoc personal and cultural assessments. Adam's hopes and
George's fears are *both* well-grounded.

Predicting the cultural values of a hypothetical group
of clients is necessarily complex, but a few observations
about pension funds are in order. Public pension funds
are suffused with the values of the political bureaucra-
cies of which they are a part. To know the larger political
culture is to understand a great deal about the culture of
the fund. In the political climate of, say, New York City,
we would be astonished to see a public pension official
revealing the slightest hint of intolerance, let alone acting on it. In our own state of North Carolina, our expectations would be quite different. Among private funds, it
is the culture of the sponsoring company that sets the
tone of the fund. Here, George's worst fears may be realized. Relationships with financial advisers are indeed

important, but these relationships are most often based on traditional male-bonding activities such as golf, hockey games, and expensive steak dinners leavened with dirty jokes.

As anthropologists, however, we don't think that it is either economically necessary or morally justifiable for financial organizations to conform to the meaner aspects of their clients' cultures. The *pandering-to-the-customer* defense is nothing new. Elite law firms long justified their exclusion of women and minorities by saying, "We'd like to, but the clients wouldn't stand for it." But firms did begin to diversify, and the clients stood for it. The clients continue to complain about the price and quality of the work but not about the race and gender of the people doing it. On the contrary, the firms that once dragged their feet now pay a heavy price in recruiting talent with attendant consequences for their work product.

Perhaps the law firms simply underestimated their clients, which suggests that George may be doing the same. But perhaps these firms *really* underestimated their own capacity to lead and influence. When law firms or financial advisers or advertisers or television producers raise the pandering-to-the-customer defense, they implicitly argue that they are only responding to cultural values that they are powerless to change. Institutions do influence one another, however, and those that are willing to exercise leadership can shape cultural values rather than merely reflect them.

Kirkham McDowell, in the person of George, has been presented with an opportunity for leadership. We believe that the firm is morally bound to seize that opportunity. The history of elite law firms suggests that, in the long run, the moral choice will be the lucrative one as well.

When major changes in cultural values take place, it pays to be leading the trend rather than running behind making excuses.

MICHAEL R. LOSEY, *a certified Senior Professional in Human Resources, is the president and CEO of the Society for Human Resource Management in Alexandria, Virginia. He has also served for more than 28 years in human resource management and has held executive-level positions at two* Fortune 500 *organizations.*

Adam has already made a thoughtful and important decision. Unfortunately, George and the management of Kirkham McDowell do not seem prepared to deal with the issue of sexual orientation in the workplace, though one could assume that sooner or later it would demand attention. The question is, can George and Kirkham McDowell, in the void created by their own lack of direction, live with Adam's actions?

If Kirkham McDowell intends to compete in a world where the level of success or failure depends on the skills and abilities of an increasingly diverse global work force, the answer must be a resounding yes. In fact, the firm's managers should not only support Adam's decision but also use this opportunity to reexamine their own assumptions and competitive practices. They will find that many employers have adopted policies on this issue. A recent poll of human resource professionals, conducted by the Society for Human Resource Management, showed that more than 65% of the 145 people surveyed work for companies that have well-understood policies against employment discrimination based on sexual orientation.

Struggling to manage without an explicit policy, George is wrestling with the same kind of issues raised a few decades ago when the public began debating the proper treatment of women and minorities in the work force. Anyone who worked in a personnel office in those days (before we had human resource departments) can remember when women were expected to resign when their pregnancies became visible or when African-American candidates were often at a disadvantage despite their qualifications and abilities. And it wasn't so long ago that airlines employed only female flight attendants because passengers supposedly preferred to be served by women.

By breaking down barriers for women and minorities in the workplace, we have learned that a policy of inclusion results in more creativity, greater productivity, and a larger applicant pool from which to draw qualified candidates. That's why it is so important to eliminate barriers that keep people out of the work force for reasons unrelated to their basic abilities. In fact, the longer an organization takes to recognize these barriers and eliminate them, the more that organization is at risk.

It simply makes good managerial sense to identify and utilize the best qualified people to support and improve an organization's competitive status. If George steps back and views his decision from that standpoint, the solution becomes clear. Adam has a proven track record of success. There can be little doubt of his value to the organization, especially when we recall that Adam is not to attend the dinner simply as a guest, but as a guest of honor for his efforts on behalf of the firm.

If George tells Adam that he may *not* bring his partner to the dinner, Adam may decide to leave Kirkham McDowell and join a competitor. If Adam does stay under those circumstances, chances are that the emotions surrounding the issue will build and affect his attitude toward his job, his performance, as well as the opinions and morale of fellow workers. Either option is a heavy price to pay. When all is said and done, does George really believe that companies doing business with his firm care more about Adam's sexual orientation than how he has helped them succeed? And doesn't George realize that in his desire to protect the firm's business with certain clients, he may jeopardize future business with other clients?

Even if the worst case scenario occurs and certain clients object to Adam's continued involvement simply because of his sexual orientation, Kirkham McDowell's decision to study the issue and determine a policy will ultimately prove useful. And if the organization is steadfast in its support of Adam, the majority of clients will accept its decision sooner or later. They may even learn something in the process.

CHARLES COLBERT *is a management consultant in strategic human resources and work-force diversity in Cambridge, Massachusetts.*
JOHN WOFFORD *is a lawyer and mediator at ENDISPUTE, Inc., in Boston. They are coauthors of "Sexual Orientation in the Workplace: The Strategic Challenge,"* Compensation & Benefits Management, *Summer 1993.*

It's important to understand the developing legal context of this case. In April 1993, Minnesota became the eighth state to outlaw discrimination based on sexual orientation, joining California, Connecticut, Hawaii, Massachusetts, New Jersey, Vermont, Wisconsin, and the District of Columbia. A number of governors have addressed the subject by issuing executive orders covering public employment. And more than 100 cities have similar ordinances, including St. Louis, where Kirkham McDowell is located. In fact, the board of aldermen in St. Louis added sexual orientation to its list of protected minority categories—race, religion, age, gender, national origin, and disability—in October, 1992. Adam is thus legally protected from discrimination in all the terms, conditions, and privileges of his employment. Admittedly, however, no one would start a lawsuit solely over the dinner issue.

More than 70 million Americans are now covered by these laws, orders, and ordinances that seek to protect homosexuals from discriminatory action. Under these laws, sexual orientation is irrelevant to the entire range of employment activities from hiring to firing.

As such, sexuality is a private matter, and Adam is not flaunting his orientation by discussing it with George. He is merely presenting himself in his entirety. His sexual orientation is just as much a part of him as color or religion or national origin is a part of any other person. We would not accuse the light-skinned African-American who had "passed" as white and the Jewish person with a "gentile" name of flaunting, if they later chose to reveal their true selves. We would call it courage and honesty. And gay people who come out of the closet are at last gaining the courage to be honest in precisely the same way.

Right now, George and Adam need to think through the social dynamics of the banquet and its aftermath. Will spouses of other employees be recognized from the platform? If so, Adam will want his partner to be treated similarly. And now that the firm officially knows that Adam has a domestic partner, Robert's name should appear in the firm directory if spouses of heterosexual employees appear. Corporate America, albeit slowly, is getting used to "Mr. and Mr." and "Ms. and Ms."

As an openly gay couple, we have experienced this crumbling of discriminatory walls firsthand. Yes, we initially faced a barrier of discomfort, as well as our own ambivalence about raising the issue. For a time, when attending workplace and client functions together, we felt somewhat on display. But by taking the initiative ourselves in a non-threatening way, we all—ourselves, employers, and clients—were able to adjust to this new social dimension in business.

Undoubtedly, some Kirkham McDowell employees and clients will demonstrate strongly held objections to homosexuality. George needs to prepare carefully for this issue. Everyone is entitled to his or her moral views on issues of sexuality, but they should be checked at the office door. The workplace should be an essentially secular environment. Just as people work side by side with others who may hold different beliefs about and engage in different practices concerning divorce, abortion, premarital sex, contraception, interracial marriage, or the use of alcohol, so people who differ fundamentally on the issue of homosexuality can get along and work together productively. Acceptable behavior, not acceptable beliefs, is the appropriate workplace standard.

ELIZABETH MCNAMARA *is a member of the law firm of Lankenau Kovner & Kurtz in New York and cochairs the board of the Lambda Legal Defense and Education Fund.*

Though George Campbell may not realize it, Adam Lawson has very politely presented him with an ultimatum: either immediately accept his decision to be open about his sexuality or eventually accept his resignation. What George must decide is whether or not his fears about the consequences of Adam's declaration are more

important than the contribution Adam makes to
Kirkham McDowell Securities. To do that, George will
have to examine his own assumptions, prejudices, and
insularity. Why, for example, would he think that
Adam—obviously an ambitious, successful professional
whose judgment has already carried him far—would
turn up at an important event with someone he just met
at the gym? Because even if he knows better intellectu-
ally, George's gut response to a situation that makes him
uncomfortable is to think of homosexual stereotypes:
desperate, lonely people unable to sustain important
relationships. Why is a lover of five years not like a wife
of five years? The difference is only in the eye of the heterosexual beholder.

George must also understand that if he decides to
support Adam's decision, there is no way to foresee,
much less to control, people's reactions. He may experience, in a small way, what gay people who are open
about their sexuality face every day. What impact does
this information, aired publicly, have on my life? What
decisions are made? What promotion or raise didn't I
get? What gossip goes on?

George must have the courage of his convictions. He
might want to tell his superior, but he must consider
what he will do if ordered to rein Adam in. As for clients,
if they are going to bolt over a gay companion, it seems
unlikely that they were a solid bet to begin with.

Originally published in July–August 1993
Reprint 93411

About the Contributors

ROBIN J. ELY is an Associate Professor at the Harvard Business School. She investigates how organizations can better manage their race and gender relations while at the same time increasing their effectiveness. Her research in this area focuses on learning and organizational change with attention to conflict, power, and social identity.

JOYCE K. FLETCHER is Professor of Management at the Center for Gender in Organizations at the Simmons Graduate School of Management in Boston and a Senior Research Scholar at the Jean Baker Miller Training Institute at the Wellesley College Centers for Women. She uses relational theory to study a wide range of workplace issues and teaches courses in organizational behavior, power, and leadership. She is the author of *Disappearing Acts*, as well as *Beyond Work-Family Balance*, written with colleagues Rhona Rapoport, Lotte Bailyn, and Bettye Pruitt, which details an action research methodology for achieving "small wins" in the workplace.

ALDEN M. HAYASHI is a Senior Editor with the *Harvard Business Review*. He has more than fifteen years of publishing experience covering the areas of science and high technology. Before joining *HBR*, he was a member of the board of editors for *Scientific American*, where he wrote and edited articles on computer science, physics, and mathematics. He was also Executive Editor of *Datamation*, a monthly computer trade magazine for information-technology professionals.

DOUGLAS M. MCCRACKEN is the CEO of Deloitte Consulting, one of the world's leading consulting firms. He is also Chairman of Deloitte & Touche LLP in the United States. Mr. McCracken has been an established leader in the consulting industry for more than twenty years, and has been recognized by *Consulting Magazine* as one of the profession's most influential consultants of 1999 and 2001 and as one of the industry's top five leaders. In 1999 the *Larry King Cardiac Foundation* named him "Man of the Year." He has been featured in many of the most influential international business publications as a spokesman for the consulting industry.

DEBRA E. MEYERSON is a Visiting Professor of Organizational Behavior at Stanford University's Graduate School of Business and at the Center for Work, Technology, and Organization within Stanford's School of Engineering. She is also affiliated faculty at the Center for Gender in Organizations at the Simmons Graduate School of Management and at Stanford's Center for Social Innovation and Center for Comparative Study of Race and Ethnicity. Professor Meyerson has given seminars for companies and non-profit organizations throughout the world, and has been an advisor and director on the boards of the journal *Organization*, Pacific Crest Outward Bound School, Women of Silicon Valley, 20% by 2020, and East Palo Alto Young Women's Entrepreneurship Project. She was selected as one of the Bay Area's "seventy-five most influential women in business" by the *San Francisco Business Times* and has been the recipient of a number of awards and grants, most recently from the Ford Foundation. She has published more than thirty articles and chapters in scholarly and applied publications, and is the author of *Tempered Radicals*.

At the time this article was originally published, ROBERT SCHRANK was the author of two additional *HBR* articles, as well as the author of a book based on his lifelong work experiences, *Ten Thousand Working Days.*

DAVID A. THOMAS is Professor of Organizational Behavior and Human Resources Management at Harvard Business School. Professor Thomas is a noted authority on the challenges of managing and mentoring a diverse work force, minority executive development, self-assessment, and career development. His recent book, *Breaking Through*, coauthored with John J. Gabarro, has been hailed by the *Boston Globe* as "A massive primer for professionals seeking to understand success and employers who wish to foster diversity in their upper ranks." He is the winner of numerous research awards, including the Academy of Management George R. Terry 2001 Book Award and the Executive Development Roundtable Marion Gislason Award for contribution to the theory and practice of executive development.

R. ROOSEVELT THOMAS, JR., CEO of R. Thomas Consulting & Training, Inc., has been at the forefront of developing and implementing innovative strategies for maximizing organizational and individual potential for over two decades. He is also Founder and President of the American Institute for Managing Diversity, Inc., a research, public policy, and education enterprise with the objective of fostering effective management of diversity. In his research, Dr. Thomas applies a diversity framework to issues such as the management of change, functional coordination, the integration of multiple lines of business, and acquisitions and mergers. Dr. Thomas is the author of four published books: *Redefining Diversity*, *Beyond Race and Gender*, *Building a House for Diversity*, and *Differences Do Make a Difference*. He is also the author of several articles and contributes to numerous periodicals and trade publications. In addition to his writing, Dr. Thomas has developed a series of videotapes and is a frequent speaker at national conferences and industry seminars. Dr. Thomas has been recognized by the *Wall Street Journal* as one of the top ten consultants in the country and cited by *Human Resource Executive* as one of HR's Most Influential People. In 1995, he received the American Society for Training and Development Award. He has acted as a consultant to numerous *Fortune* 500 companies, corporations, professional firms, government entities, non-profit organizations, and academic institutions.

At the time this article was originally published, ALISTAIR D. WILLIAMSON was an Editor at the Harvard Business School Press.

Index